IMAGES
of America

PHILADELPHIA JAZZ

This image of Billy Eckstine and Billie Holiday was taken at the Earle Theatre on April 20, 1946. (Photograph by John W. Mosley, courtesy of Charles L. Blockson Afro-American Collection, Temple University Libraries.)

On the Cover: Jimmy Smith, an organist from Norristown, Pennsylvania, revolutionized the use of the Hammond B-3 organ, fusing jazz and 1960s soul music. Pictured is Smith performing in Philadelphia at WJMJ Radio Station's studio in the St. James Hotel at 1226-32 Walnut Street, c. 1950s. (Photograph by John W. Mosley, courtesy of the Charles L. Blockson Afro-American Collection, Temple University Libraries.)

IMAGES
of America

PHILADELPHIA JAZZ

Suzanne Cloud, PhD, and Diane Turner, PhD

Foreword by Terell Stafford

Introduction by Bob Perkins

ARCADIA
PUBLISHING

ISBN 978-1-4671-0784-6

Published by Arcadia Publishing
Charleston, South Carolina

Library of Congress Control Number: 2022941278

For all general information, please contact Arcadia Publishing:
Telephone 843-853-2070
Fax 843-853-0044
E-mail sales@arcadiapublishing.com
For customer service and orders:
Toll-Free 1-888-313-2665

Visit us on the Internet at www.arcadiapublishing.com

Contents

Acknowledgments

First, a sincere thank-you to Serkaddis Alemayehu, instructional design and technology specialist, Charles L. Blockson Afro-American Collection, for her guidance, perseverance, attentiveness, and patience in the preparation of this volume. We are forever indebted to her. We thank Charles L. Blockson, curator emeritus, who amassed one of our nation's premier African American research centers. Special thanks to Leslie Willis-Lowry, archivist, Blockson Collection, for providing easy access to the photographic collections of John W. Mosley; Aslaku Berhanu, librarian; photographers Bruce Turner and Bill May; and the late Robert "Bootsie" Barnes. We are much obliged to other colleagues at Temple University, including Terell Stafford, chair of instrumental studies; Laura H. Carnell, professor, Boyer College of Music and Dance; Bob Perkins, radio personality, WRTI; and Brenda Galloway-Wright, associate archivist, Special Collections Research Center. We also thank Lovett Hines, artistic director/founder of the Music Education Program; Philadelphia Clef Club; and photographers Paul Somerville, H. Alonzo Jennings, L. David Hinton, and Pedro J. Matos for their contributions. Many thanks go to archivist Jack McCarthy, from the Philadelphia Jazz Legacy Project, and graphic designer Kathy Ridl for their help with the images and research. We wish to acknowledge some of the other jazz musicians who were important contributors to Philadelphia's jazz history, including trumpeter Bill Massey (1926–1966), drummer Charles "Specs" Wright (1927–1963), bassist Nelson Boyd (1928–1985), tenor saxophonist Rahsaan Roland Kirk (1935–1977), and tenor saxophonist Charles "Charlie" Cunningham (1935–2018), and many others. We dedicate this book to all the musicians, fans, entrepreneurs, and educators who built this historic jazz community, and those jazz musicians presently active who are keeping jazz alive for the future!

Foreword

I have great respect for these two authors. Both scholars in this music, they have demonstrated their support of the music and authenticity of where it comes from as it relates to Philadelphia. Suzanne Cloud, a jazz musician, author, and educator, is known for her work with Jazz Bridge, providing opportunities and support for musicians. Diane Turner, author and historian, is a huge supporter of this music and these musicians, educating present and future musicians as curator of the Charles L. Blockson Afro-American Collection at Temple University.

This book, Images of America: *Philadelphia Jazz*, gives insight into some of the early foundations of the rich history Philadelphia jazz holds. Communicating the powerful impact of jazz in Philadelphia and its impact on the world, this book speaks to where Philadelphia jazz has come from and inspires where it can go.

As a musician and educator in Philadelphia, my roots run deep here. I had the great honor and privilege to play with and know some of Philadelphia's great musicians. Their contributions and those that came before them have had a great impact on me personally and professionally and reflect the family feeling of Philadelphia, the "City of Brotherly Love." Jimmy Heath and the Heath Brothers, Shirley Scott, McCoy Tyner, Tony Williams, Benny Golson, Bootsie Barnes, Larry McKenna, Jimmy Oliver, Arthur Harper, Mickey Rocker, Bobby Durham, Joe Wilder, Johnny Coles, Trudy Pitts, Kenny Barron, Sam Dockery, and so many others would be proud of what Philadelphia music has become, and the efforts of Suzanne and Diane show respect and provide a voice to the origins of this music in Philadelphia. This is an intriguing and thoughtful glimpse into the past.

—Terell Stafford
Director of Jazz Studies and Chair of Instrumental Studies, Temple University
Artistic Director of Jazz for the Philly POPS
Managing and Artistic Director of the Philly POPS Jazz Orchestra of Philadelphia

INTRODUCTION

The city of Philadelphia is well-known because it is the home of the Liberty Bell, cheese steaks, hoagies, and soft pretzels and the breeding ground for great jazz artists. But even among the most selective jazz entrepreneurs, there may be some missing pieces in the history of this artform in Philly.

Well now, this publication, Images of America: *Philadelphia Jazz*, written by two astute authors, should fill in historical spaces for both the knowledgeable and the freshman.

The comradeship of Philly's jazz artistry lies in Philly saxophonist Benny Golson's urging his boss, Art Blakey, to hire three Philadelphians—including himself—to revamp the Blakey Quintet. This was no outright favoritism of friends, because Golson just worked with these musicians before and knew they could handle the job. This local comradery was mentioned to me by drummer Granville William "Mickey" Rocker, who explained that when he moved to Philly from the South and posed musical questions to John Coltrane, Benny Golson, and other local jazz musicians who had been around longer, they were always anxious to offer him advice. I asked Mickey if he considered this comradery a token of Philly's slogan of "Brotherly Love," he smilingly said: "Hey, you got it!"

The next time readers of this publication get involved in discussions about which city has the greatest jazz artists, they should not forget, that for a couple of decades, Philly was the "Jazz Organ Capital of the World," with Jimmy Smith, Charles Earland, Jimmy McGriff, Shirley Scott, and a handful of other B-3 artists leading the charge. And that Norristown's Jimmy Smith came to Philly to jam with other growing jazz greats, and he—like many of them—became legends of the modern jazz genre. And do not leave out the fact that the great trumpeter from Wilmington, Delaware, Clifford Brown, was a regular visitor to Philly to help hone his talent by mixing and sharing with local great names-to-be.

This book, authored by writer, jazz musician, and educator Dr. Suzanne Cloud and Dr. Diane Turner, historian, author, and curator of the Charles Blockson Afro-American Collection at Temple University, is a fine description of the jazz history in Philadelphia; this book will take you to its beginning and interestingly coax you forward.

—Bob Perkins
Longtime jazz radio host with WRTI and WHYY,
Writer and historian,
and Philadelphia Music Alliance's Walk of Fame awardee

One

Some Forerunners of Philadelphia Jazz

Surprising to many, Philadelphia jazz has roots in the mid-19th century. Francis "Frank" Johnson (1792–1844), composer, arranger, educator, orchestral conductor, music publisher, and impresario, led one of the most popular all-Black brass bands in the country. He maintained ensembles from 1812 until his death, and his compositions were popularly played through the 1930s. Raised in Philadelphia's vibrant, free Black community, Johnson participated in or his music was played for emancipation celebrations, ceremonial affairs, dances, parades, and special holidays. Johnson, a self-taught musician, was a multi-instrumentalist, proficient on the violin and a virtuoso on the Royal Kent bugle. Later, he would add the cornet and trumpet as his solo instruments. He rose to prominence around 1815 as a fine section player, and by 1818, he was a member of the newly formed Matt Black's All-Negro Marching Band in Philadelphia. In the early 1820s, Johnson formed his own band, made up primarily of woodwinds, and it became renowned in Philadelphia's upper-class circles. In fact, he was one of the first Black bandleaders to perform at integrated public concerts. Johnson wrote more than 300 compositions and was one of the first to publish sheet music. He is also credited with being the first major bandmaster in the United States to tour Europe in 1837. Dissatisfied with the limited opportunities for Black musicians in the United States and disturbed with the rising popularity of grotesque stereotypes utilized in blackface minstrelsy like Jim Crow and Zip Coon, he traveled abroad to improve his musical opportunities and knowledge. While in Britain, he played at Buckingham Palace for Queen Victoria, who presented him with a silver bugle.

Charles Luckeyth "Luckey" Roberts (1887–1968), a piano virtuoso, composer, singer, and dancer, was regarded as one of the founders of the Harlem stride piano school. Born in Philadelphia, Roberts performed on stage at the age of three and later in circus orchestras and minstrel shows. During World War I, he served in James Reese Europe's 369th Infantry "Hellfighters" band and platoon. His friends and colleagues included James P. Johnson, Fats Waller, Eubie Blake, and Willie "The Lion" Smith. Robert's ragtime and stride piano playing influenced not only his colleagues but also Duke Ellington and others. His works included the major ragtime hits "Junk Man Rag" (1913), "Railroad Blues" (1916), and "Pork and Beans" (1917). His composition "Ripples of the Nile" (1916) was recorded by bandleader Glenn Miller in 1942 and renamed "Moonlight Cocktail." Roberts was a prolific composer, penning 14 musical comedy scores and several concert works.

Instrumentalist, composer, and arranger Francis "Frank" Johnson was America's first international Black music superstar. He was the first African American to have his compositions published as sheet music (over 200), and his popularity rivaled white bands touring at the time. When his Philadelphia brass band toured England in 1837, Johnson was the first African American to tour Europe. Queen Victoria asked him to play for her, and after the concert, she presented him with a silver bugle. (Courtesy of Charles L. Blockson Afro-American Collection, Temple University Libraries.)

Johnson's marches, cotillions, operatic airs, ballads, quadrilles, quicksteps, and other forms of ballroom music were uniquely different from the traditional European melodies in that he combined the romanticism of the age with the popularity of the dance tunes of the day. His American originals were immediately adopted by other bands. By the time "Johnson's March" was published in 1815, he had created and defined the military music of America. (Courtesy of the Free Library of Philadelphia, Sheet Music Collection.)

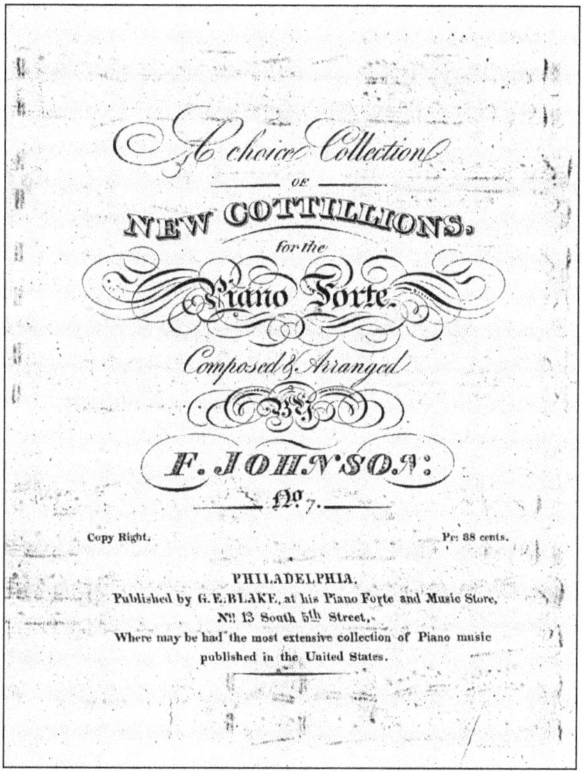

A Choice Collection of New Cotillions, for the Piano Forte Composed & Arranged by F. Johnson was published in 1824 for General Lafayette's visit and ball held at the New Theatre on Chestnut Street near Sixth Street in Philadelphia. The music, performed by Johnson's Military Band, used familiar melodies from many sources to enliven his music for dancers. He adopted tempos popular with dancers from early Spanish immigrants in 1808 and originally combined them with African and Amerindian elements. (Courtesy of Charles L. Blockson Afro-American Collection, Temple University Libraries.)

Johnson was impressed with Gen. John Cadwalader, a Quaker and a commander of Pennsylvania troops during the American Revolutionary War. General Cadwalader was with General Washington at Valley Forge. Francis Johnson composed this piece, which is one of the earliest compositions written by an American composer for the Kent bugle. (Courtesy of the Free Library of Philadelphia, Sheet Music Collection.)

Luckey Roberts (1887–1868), a composer and stride pianist born in Philadelphia, prevailed as king of the Harlem ragtime pianists, dominating many of Harlem's gladiatorial cutting contests with his lifelong friends Willie "The Lion" Smith, James P. Johnson, and Eubie Blake. By the age of five, Roberts was in show business, performing as a singer, dancer, and juggler in various shows such as *Uncle Tom's Cabin*, and he toured with two different vaudeville groups: Gus Seeke's Pickaninnies and Mayme Remington and Her Black Buster Brownie Ethiopian Prodigies. When Luckey was 10, he had already toured Europe three times. He was also a member of James Reese Europe's 369th Infantry "Hellfighters" band during World War I. He is pictured around 1920. (Courtesy of the International Center of Photography.)

"Railroad Blues," composed by Luckey Roberts in 1920, was one of his best-known blues-style rags. His rhythmic left hand and his dexterous right hand fully illustrated the breadth of his expertise and brilliance. In the 1920s, Roberts teamed up with lyricist Alex C. Rogers and cowrote three Broadway musicals, *Go-Go* (1923), *Sharlee* (1923) and *My Magnolia* (1926), the latter of which starred Adelaide Hall, a major Black revue star. (Courtesy of Charles L. Blockson Afro-American Collection, Temple University Libraries.)

Robert's "Moonlight Cocktail" (1916), developed out of his work "Ripples of the Nile," later became a bestselling hit for the Glenn Miller Orchestra during 1942. Lyrics were written by Kim Gannon, who compared the development of a romantic relationship to the mixing of an alcoholic drink. (Courtesy of Charles L. Blockson Afro-American Collection, Temple University Libraries.)

"Pork and Beans" (1913) and "Junk Man Rag" (1913) are two of the first major ragtime hits ever recorded. These compositions by Luckey Roberts have been covered by many ensembles both Black and White over the years, and one of the best versions was by Willie "The Lion" Smith on his album *Music on My Mind*. During the 1940s, Roberts opened a nightclub in Harlem called Luckey's Rendezvous. (Courtesy of the Free Library of Philadelphia, Sheet Music Collection.)

Two

Organizing and Improvising

Musicians' Protective Union Local 274, American Federation of Musicians (AFM), was chartered on January 2, 1935, becoming one of the more than 50 Black unions to emerge in the AFM during a period of segregation. Prior to its establishment in 1916, Local Branch No. 591 of the AFM, a subsidiary of White Local 77, was "formed for the purpose to bring the Negro musicians of the city more closely together and to form a uniform rate of pay to the musicians and for the mutual benefit of musicians."

Frank Thurman "Frankie" Fairfax, orchestra leader, composer, and trumpeter, migrated to Philadelphia in 1933 and became a key figure in the organizing of Local 274. His orchestra settled in Philadelphia and needed union cards to perform. Fairfax visited AFM's International headquarters, where it was recommended for him to secure at least 75 musicians to establish a new Black local. He was assisted by orchestra leader Raymond Smith, founder of the Rhythm Club, who encouraged his members of mostly profession musicians to join.

During the 1960s, the AFM was targeted as one of the most segregated affiliates in the AFL-CIO. The AFM's decision was to merge locals in the same jurisdiction. Consequently, Black unions were being submerged with White unions. Local 274's position was that they were integrated and saw no benefits in being submerged with Local 77, hence became the last independent Black local in the AFM. Therefore, the AFM canceled Local 274's charter effective April 1, 1971. In other cities where the Black locals were forced to merge, the White locals gained control of their assets. This was not the case in Philadelphia.

The Philadelphia Clef Club was officially incorporated on December 21, 1966, as a Pennsylvania non-profit organization. Local 274 transferred its assets into their social club, including their building, which was located at 912 South Broad Street; their private liquor license; and all musicians' funds. In 1970, the city declared eminent domain over their building. The Clef Club was moved to 13th and Washington Streets and ultimately a new facility at 736 South Broad Street.

First Annual Concert and Reception

OF

MUSICIANS' PROTECTIVE UNION

Local 591, American Federation of Musicians at the

Waltz Dream Academy, : : 13th above Jefferson St.

Tuesday Eve., May 15, 1917

Doors open at 7.30 Concert 8:30 Dancing 10 to 2

Having such a large number of musicians to choose from, the committee will present Special Orchestras which will make this feature unequalled by any event this season.

Admission 50 Cents

Philadelphia's first Black musicians' union, Local 591, was formed in the fall of 1916 and was located at 1441 Carpenter Street. Its first annual concert and reception was held at Waltz Dream Hall, 1520 North Thirteenth Street, on May 26, 1917, with tenor Sterling Ray, soprano Mayme Fletcher, violinist Joshua Sadler, and the Charles Taylor Jazz Band. (Courtesy of the *Philadelphia Tribune*.)

Bandleader and violinist Raymond L. Smith (1896–1967), one of the founders of Local 274, was well versed in symphony and chamber music, blues, jazz, and a variety of popular music forms. He is pictured at left with Charles McCabe (at right) at the Academy of Music around the 1940s. In 1945, Smith founded Dra Mu Opera Company. (Photograph by John W. Mosley, courtesy of Charles L. Blockson Afro-American Collection, Temple University Libraries.)

Frank Fairfax, secretary of Local 274, is seated at his desk in the union building around 1960. Fairfax attended West Virginia State College, graduated with a business degree, and studied music under Clarence Cameron White. He was a bandleader, musician, music arranger, and songwriter, performing in Philadelphia and other northeastern cities. (Courtesy of Cyd Mathias.)

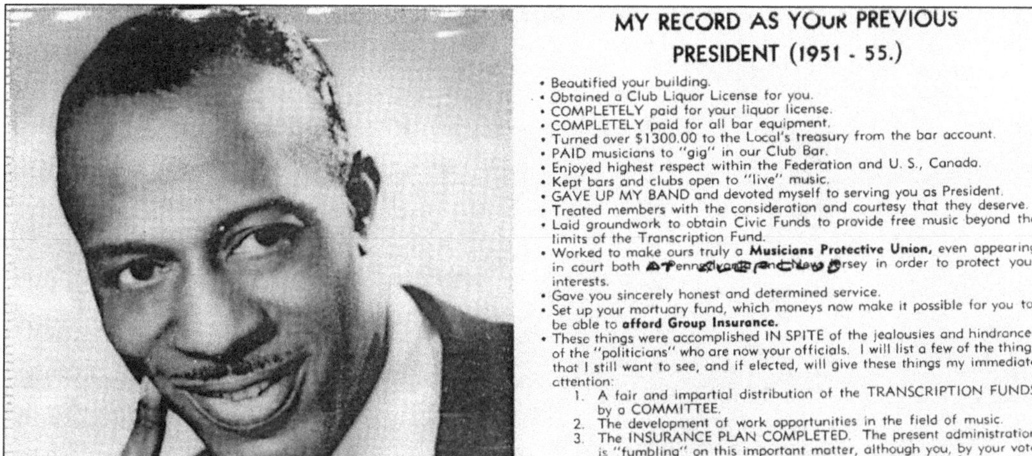

Pictured is a James Euclid "Jimmy" Adams campaign flyer from 1959. Under Adams's leadership, the Philadelphia Clef Club was established to promote and to advance projects for the benefit of jazz musicians. He was president of Local 274 when the union's charter was cancelled. (Courtesy of Diane D. Turner.)

James Euclid "Jimmy" Adams (1908–1998), the president of Musicians' Protective Union Local 274, is pictured at the 54th Convention of the American Federation of Musicians in New York City in June 1951. The convention was held every year from 1896 except for two years during World War II. (Courtesy of Diane D. Turner.)

Pictured here are Local 274 officials at the 57th Annual Convention in Milwaukee, Wisconsin, in 1954. Local 274 was the second largest Black AFM local. Black musicians were barred from the then-segregated white Philadelphia Local 77. From left to right are Selmer Payne, Pres. Jimmy Adams, and Secretary Henry Lowe. (Courtesy of Winston Lowe.)

Pictured here are Local 274 officials at the 59th Annual Convention in Atlantic City, New Jersey, in 1956. From left to right are Sec. Henry Lowe, Del. Franklin Walker, and Pres. Jimmy Shorter. (Courtesy of Winston Lowe.)

The former union building at 912 South Broad Street became the mecca for jazz in Philadelphia where musicians like Duke Ellington, Sarah Vaughn, Count Basie, Sonny Stitt, Max Roach, and many other musicians could relax, jam, socialize, and exchange artistic ideas. On weekends, the union was packed with jazz lovers who came to hear the music and watch the celebrities. (Courtesy of City of Philadelphia, Department of Records.)

Henry Lowe, secretary of Local 274, is shown at his desk at the union building located at 900 South Broad Street around the 1940s. (Courtesy of Winston Lowe.)

Tenor saxophonist Bootsie Barnes takes a break from his duties as Local 274's assistant secretary outside of the union hall. Pres. James E. Adams encouraged him to run for the position. Bootsie's uncle and mentor Jimmy Hamilton played clarinet for Duke Ellington. Bootsie became a formidable musical presence in Philadelphia, playing with Shirley Scott, Jimmy Smith, and many others. (Courtesy of the Charles L. Blockson Afro-American Collection, Temple University Libraries.)

Pictured from left to right around the 1940s are Local 274 officials George "Doc" Hyder and James "Jimmy" Shorter (1903–1982). Doc Hyder, the first elected president of Local 274 (January 6, 1935), organized his orchestra and his Twelve Famous Southernaires, a popular jazz band from the early 1920s to mid-1930s. By 1938, the union had 360 members in good standing. Jimmy Shorter was president in 1956. He headed his own band and worked as a musical therapist. (Photograph by John W. Mosley, courtesy of Charles L. Blockson Afro-American Collection, Temple University Libraries.)

Trombonist Al Grey performs at Local 77 around the 1960s. Growing up in Pottstown, Pennsylvania, he started playing trombone in a band called Goodwill Boys, led by his father. After World War II, he joined Benny Carter's band, then the bands of Jimmie Lunceford, Lucky Millinder, and Lionel Hampton. In the 1950s, he played in Dizzy Gillespie and Count Basie's big bands. (Courtesy of Diane D. Turner.)

Local 274 members are pictured at the 30th anniversary in 1965. From left to right are (first row) Treasurer Leroy McCoy, Vice Pres. Basil Jackson, Pres. James E. Adams, and Sec. Frank Fairfax; (second row) two unidentified members, Othello Curry, Franklin E. Walker, and John T. Brown. (Courtesy of the Philadelphia Clef Club of Jazz and Performing Arts.)

The Philadelphia Clef Club of Jazz & the Performing Arts is pictured in 1995 at a new facility built on the corner of Broad and Fitzwater Streets. In 1982, Dr. Bernard C. Watson, former president of the William Penn Foundation, allocated funds for construction of the new building at 736 South Broad Street. This was the first facility ever constructed specifically as a jazz institution—a testament to the nation's history. (Courtesy of the Philadelphia Clef Club.)

Three

PLACES TO BE, MUSICIANS TO SEE

World War I and the Great Migration energized the popularity of big bands and orchestras to accommodate a rising urban Black population hungry for entertainment. Despite segregation, Black entrepreneur John T. Gibson owned Gibson's Theatre at Broad and Lombard Streets, where Doc Hyder, who was known as a master of syncopation, was a fixture with his orchestra. Gibson also owned the Standard Theatre at 1126 South Street, where blues singer Bessie Smith performed. Black creators and innovators of jazz broke through discriminatory barriers with their music. And racism could not keep the music or the musicians apart, no matter what color. Italian American guitarist Eddie Lang was captivated by jazz and rushed to learn and play it, and later saxophonist Charlie Ventura and clarinetist Buddy DeFranco also fell under the music's spell. In 1937, violinist Jan Savitt was the first to integrate a Philadelphia band when he hired well-known singer George " Bon Bon" Tunnell to perform and record with his Top Hatters, even though Black bands were prohibited from most white clubs. One exception was Frankie Fairfax and his Campus Club Orchestra, which regularly performed at one of Philadelphia's premier white nightclubs—the Rafters Café.

Big bands were in huge demand as jazz ensembles, dubbed red hot jazz bands and later swing bands, became essential for dancing locally, nationally, and abroad. In 1925, Philadelphia pianist and arranger Sam Wooding took his orchestra and floor show to Europe on several tours, becoming one of the most popular band leaders of the era. Other bands stayed closer to home. Mme. Keene's Orchestra, Gertie Monk and Charles Taylor's Jazz Orchestra, and Rickett's 15-Piece Jazz Band were popular during the second decade of the 20th century.

In the 1930s and 1940s, trumpeter Charlie Gaines performed with many national jazz bands before he formed his big band under various names such as the Golden Dawn Orchestra and Charlie Gaines and His Stablemates. Other crowd-pleasers included Bobby Lee and His Cotton Pickers, Jimmy Adams and His Southern Swingsters, and Jimmy Gorham and His Royal Kentuckians Orchestra. Multi-instrumentalist Frankie Fairfax migrated to Philadelphia from West Virginia while playing in Edward's Collegians in 1933 and became one of the most important bandleaders in the city. He nurtured such young talents as trumpeters Dizzy Gillespie and Charlie Shavers and drummer Shadow Wilson while hiring pianist and organist Bill Doggett as his musical director to get the young lions pouring into the city in shape to change American music.

John T. Gibson (1878–1937), nicknamed "Little Giant," purchased the New Standard Theatre in 1914 at Twelfth and South Streets, which produced vaudeville shows. It was one of the finest theaters owned and managed by an African American in the United States. Seven years later, he also owned Gibson's Theater at Broad and Lombard Streets. (Courtesy of Langston Hughes Memorial Library, Lincoln University.)

Pictured are interior and exterior views of Gibson's New Standard Theatre in 1919. Gibson entertained theatergoers at the Standard and Gibson Theaters and was hailed as one of the great theatrical magnates of his day. He was listed in *Bradstreet's Register of Millionaires*. (Courtesy of Langston Hughes Memorial Library, Lincoln University.)

Bessie Smith (1894–1937), known as the "Empress of the Blues," was Columbia Recording Company's top recording artist in 1925. She regularly performed in Philadelphia and lived on Christian Street in South Philly after her marriage to Jack McGee in 1923. Shown here is an advertisement for Bessie Smith's performance at the Standard Theatre on July 10, 1930. (Courtesy of the *Philadelphia Tribune*.)

Shown here is a 1921 advertisement of one of the many affairs where pianist Gertie Monk and violinist Charles Taylor performed. Gertie Monk and Charles Taylor's Jazz Orchestra had a reputation for always performing harmonious music with sweet and jazzy airs that pleased dancers. In 1929, Gertie Monk played piano and Charles Taylor played first violin with Luckey Robert's society entertainers. (Courtesy of the *Philadelphia Tribune*.)

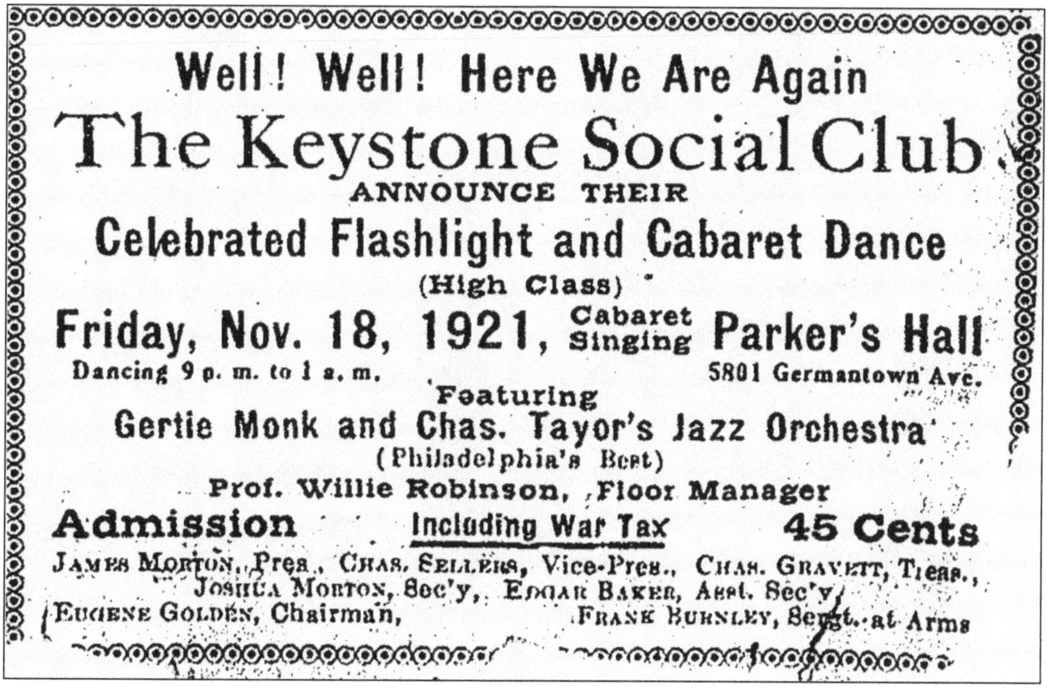

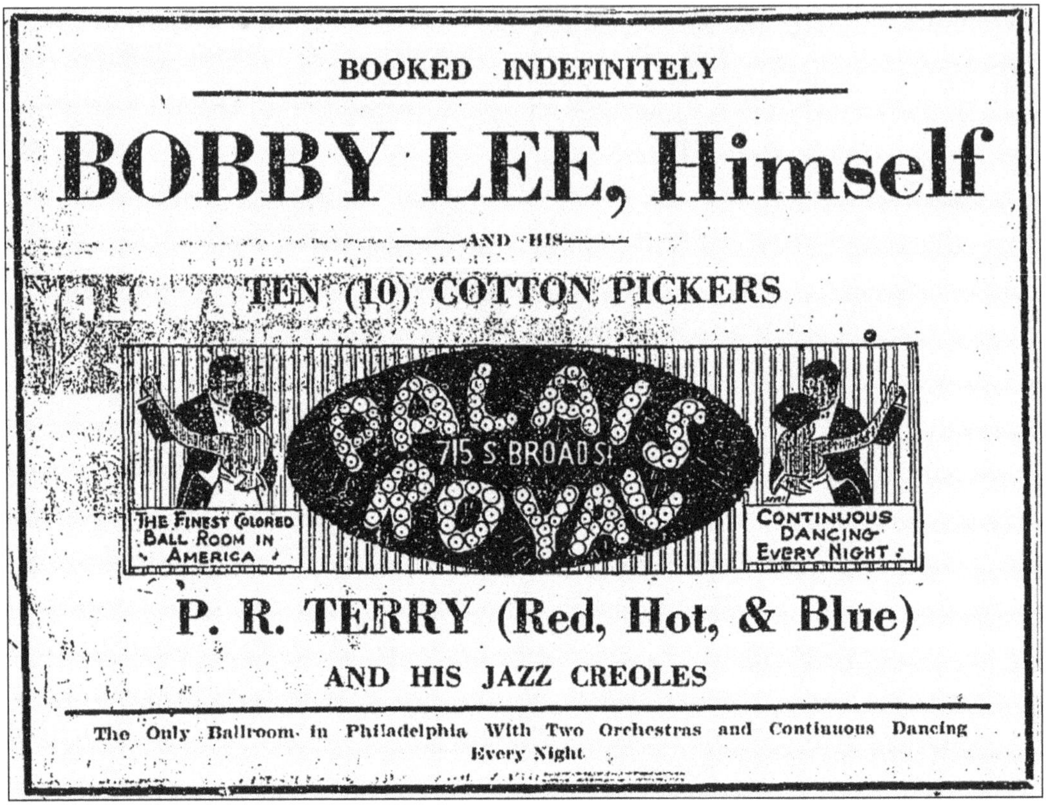

Pianist Bobby Lee's Cotton Pickers were a popular band during the 1930s. Dancing was in vogue and happening at the Palais Royal Ball Room, 715 South Broad Street, with Bobby Lee and his orchestra. He was one of the musicians that promoter Irvin Mills wanted to hire at the Cotton Club, but Lee was making so much money in Philadelphia that he declined the offer.

Pianist, arranger, and band leader Sam Wooding was born in Philadelphia in 1895 and became one of the most successful bandleaders in the 1920s and 1930s. He toured Europe many times as Sam Wooding and his Chocolate Kiddies and recorded for Columbia Records. He is shown here with his orchestra in Berlin, Germany, around 1930. (Ullstein bild/Granger–Historical Picture Archive.)

Shown here are an invitation to a Cynwyd Club event in 1932 and an announcement of the Association of Colored Engineers and Electricians' affair where pianist Mme. Io. Keene performed in 1918. She had the leading dance band in Philadelphia and was one of the top entertainment contractors in the city. When folks wanted to enjoy really good dance music, they would send for Madame Keene's Orchestra, or her company would book different bandleaders to play other jobs her ensemble couldn't. Of all the multiple gigs played by various bands on weekends in the city, many were working for Madame Keene. (Courtesy of Charles L. Blockson Afro-American Collection, Temple University Libraries, and the *Philadelphia Tribune.*)

Trumpeter and trombonist Frank Thurmond "Frankie" Fairfax (1899–1972) was a renowned bandleader, music arranger, and songwriter who migrated to Philadelphia in 1933 with a traveling band called Edward's Collegians and became a dynamic force in Philadelphia jazz. (Courtesy of Cyd Mathis.)

By the mid-1930s, the Frankie Fairfax Orchestra included organist and musical director Bill Doggett and trumpeters Dizzy Gillespie, Charlie Shavers, and Carl "Bama" Warwick. Later, clarinetist and saxophonist Jimmy Hamilton and drummer Shadow Wilson would come through his band. Fairfax composed two popular compositions, "That's What I'm Talkin' 'Bout" and "Bouncin'." (Courtesy of Cyd Mathis.)

Italian American guitarist Eddie Lang, who introduced the guitar into early white jazz bands like the Paul Whiteman Orchestra, is pictured here in *The Big Broadcast of 1936* with Bing Crosby. During the 1920s, he gave the guitar a prominence it previously lacked as a solo instrument, as part of a band or orchestra, and as accompaniment for vocalists. (Pictorial Press Ltd./Alamy Stock Photograph.)

Shown here is the album cover of *Joe Venuti & Eddie Lange Collection 1926–33*, released in 2014. Italian Americans violinist Venuti (1903–1978) and guitarist Lang (1902–1933) were considered pioneers of the use of stringed instruments in jazz. They formed the most famous violin-guitar duo in jazz a decade prior to Stéphane Grappelli and Django Reinhardt. (Courtesy of Charles L. Blockson Afro-American Collection, Temple University Libraries.)

A graduate of Tennessee State University, tenor saxophonist Jimmy Adams (1908–1998) played with many greats during the big band era, including Count Basie and Duke Ellington. Adams took over organist Harry "Doc" Bagby's band when Bagby was drafted during World War II, and later, Adams founded the Philadelphia Clef Club, the social wing of Musicians' Protective Union Local 274, American Federation of Musicians. He is pictured here in the 1940s. (Courtesy of Diane D. Turner.)

Trombonist James "Jimmie" Gorham (1903–1976) organized Jimmie Gorman and His Swing Orchestra, one of the most prestigious ensembles in the city. In 1948, his band was one of the first to play shows at Harlem's Apollo Theatre, the Baltimore Royal Theater, and Washington's Howard Theater. (Courtesy of Diane D. Turner.)

Shown here is a c. 1930s promotional photograph of maestro Morris Mosley (1909–1946). His orchestra was nominated by Musicians' Protective Union Local 274 as "Philly King of Swing" in 1939. Mosley was a famed bandleader who travelled throughout the country before settling in New York. (Courtesy of Bristol Rush.)

This 1945 advertisement announces Morris Mosley's Celebrity Club. That year, Mosley opened the club in Harlem. It was located at 35 East 125th Street and featured big-name acts and bands. The club also catered to banquets and parties. (Courtesy of the *Philadelphia Tribute*.)

Shown here are Jan Savitt's Top Hatters in the 1940s. Violinist Savitt, born in Ukraine and raised in Philadelphia, began his career in classical music with the Philadelphia Orchestra but then left to pursue jazz. He became known as "The Stokowski of Swing." In 1937, Savitt established the Top Hatters and hired George "Bon Bon" Tunnell, one of the first African American singers to perform and record with an all-white band. (Courtesy of Stan Richards.)

Shown here is vocalist George "Bon Bon" Tunnell (1903–1975). He began singing with Candy Kids and then became a member of the vocal group the Three Keyes. This popular group toured the Radio-Keith-Orpheum (RKO) theater circuit and had a long-running engagement at the Palladium in London. When the Three Keyes disbanded in 1936, Tunnell was hired by Jan Savitt for his band, the Top Hatters. As the band gained national fame, Tunnell became one of the premier attractions on recordings such as "720," "Wonderful World," "El Rancho Grande," and "I Don't Want to Set the World on Fire." (Courtesy of Diane Turner.)

Shown at right around the 1950s are Charles Howard "Charlie Old Devil" Gaines (1900–1986, left), trumpeter, band leader, and composer; trumpeter Louis Armstrong (right); and an unidentified male (back right). Below, Gaines entertains the ladies after a 1950s performance. Gaines started playing as a teenager. His first professional job was with Gertrude and Charles Taylor, and then, in 1920, he moved to New York City. Gaines played with Louis Armstrong in the 1928 edition of "Black Birds" with singer Florence Mills while becoming good friends with poet Langston Hughes. During the 1930s, Gaines returned to Philadelphia and organized his own orchestra, which performed in Philadelphia, New York, Detroit, and Atlantic City, New Jersey, at Club Harlem. He also recorded with Fats Waller, Bessie Smith, and Clarence Williams. He composed "I Can't Dance Got Ants in My Pants." (Both, photographs by John W. Mosley, courtesy of Charles L. Blockson Afro-American Collection, Temple University Libraries.)

Pictured from left to right are saxophonist George Auld (1919–1990), Lena Horne (1917–2010), and pianist Horace Henderson (1904–1988) at the Earle Theatre in 1944. Horne was an actress, singer, and civil rights activist known for her striking beauty and silky voice. She overcame profound racism on her way to becoming one of the best-known African American performers in the country. (Photograph by John W. Mosley, courtesy of the Charles L. Blockson Afro-American Collection, Temple University Libraries.)

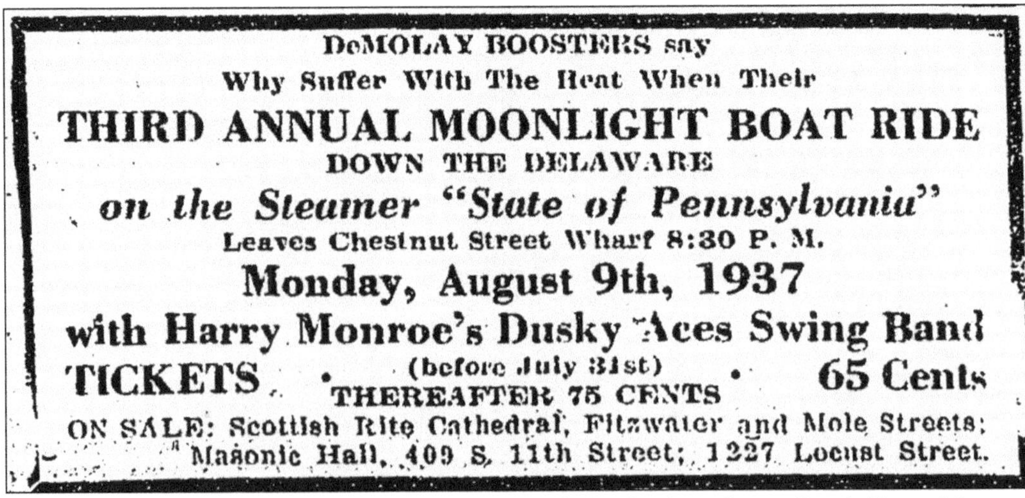

DeMOLAY BOOSTERS say
Why Suffer With The Heat When Their
THIRD ANNUAL MOONLIGHT BOAT RIDE
DOWN THE DELAWARE
on the Steamer "State of Pennsylvania"
Leaves Chestnut Street Wharf 8:30 P. M.
Monday, August 9th, 1937
with Harry Monroe's Dusky Aces Swing Band
TICKETS • (before July 31st) THEREAFTER 75 CENTS • 65 Cents
ON SALE: Scottish Rite Cathedral, Fitzwater and Mole Streets; Masonic Hall, 409 S. 11th Street; 1227 Locust Street.

This 1937 advertisement announces Harry Monroe's Dusky Aces Swing Band. Harry Monroe's band was considered a society band who played for the Black bourgeoisie. It received top dollar for performing show tunes, tangos, waltzes, and other music genres. (Courtesy of the *Philadelphia Tribune*.)

Shown here is an announcement of Henry Lowe's Carolinians performing at the Arts Café, a hot spot in North Philadelphia, in 1935. Trumpeter Henry Lowe and his orchestra were one of the hottest bands in Philadelphia. Lowe's swinging entourage ranged in size from 16 to 20 musicians. Like many of the popular bands at the time, the Carolinians played in music venues in Philadelphia and New Jersey such as the Moon Light Cabaret, the Acorn Inn, the Club Orlando, Cotton Club, and Club Harlem. (Courtesy of Winston Lowe.)

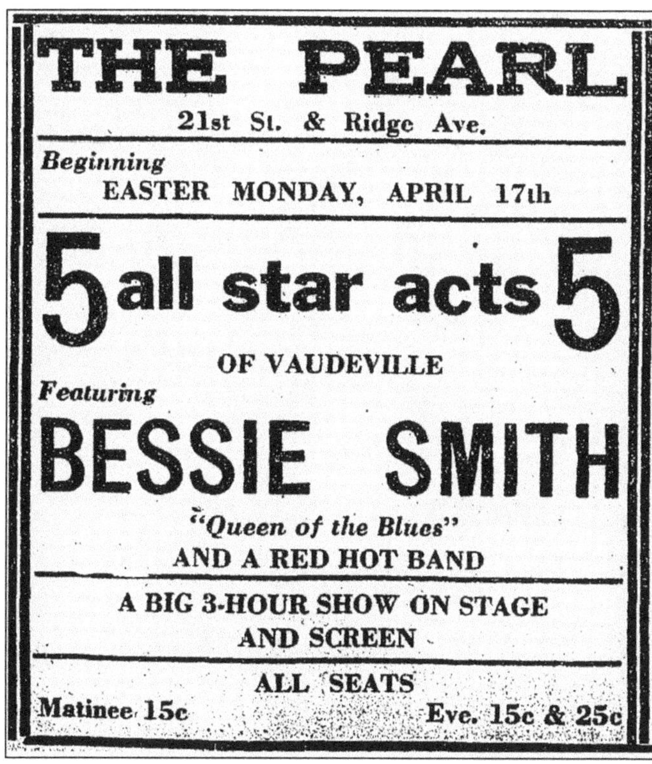

Singer Bessie Smith performed at Pearl Theatre at Twenty-First Street and Ridge Avenue in North Philadelphia in 1933. Smith frequently sang in Philadelphia. Pearl Theatre was a popular venue that had a reputation for bringing in stars such as Smith, Pearl Bailey, and Bill "Bojangles" Robinson. (Courtesy of the *Philadelphia Tribune*.)

Vocalist Ella Fitzgerald and bandleader and drummer Chick Webb sing and swing at Philadelphia's Convention Hall on October 28, 1938, sponsored by the Democratic Party. (Both photographs by John W. Mosley, courtesy of Charles L. Blockson Afro-American Collection, Temple University Libraries.)

Shown here on the left is Melvin "Sax" Gill holding his baritone along with unidentified band members around the 1950s. This popular orchestra was always composed of well-known local musicians such as drummer William Ross, trumpeter and trombonist Edwin Moore, trombonist Louis Blackburn, bassist Sidney Francis, and pianist John Johnson. (Courtesy of Diane Turner.)

This 1949 ad announces Sax Gill's All-Star Band. During January, the band played every night at Budweiser, located at Sixteenth and South Streets. The band was known to entertain patrons with popular tunes. (Courtesy of the *Philadelphia Tribune*.)

Shown here from left to right are John Ferrell (also known as Omar Bey) on bass, Daisy Mae on cocktail drum, and an unidentified guitarist around the 1950s. The band was known for bebop and R&B. Mae's group was a starting point for jazz musicians such as John Coltrane and pianist Kenny Kyle. (Courtesy of Diane Turner.)

From left to right are (sitting) Hassan and Sax Young; (standing) Johnny Ferrell, Eddie Piper, and Fred Simmons around the 1950s. James "Sax" Young, tenor saxophonist and bandleader, was an original member of Jimmy Heath's big band, formed in 1946. At that time, Heath said that Sax played better than Benny Golson and John Coltrane, who were also members of his big band. Later, Sax formed a trio. (Courtesy of Diane Turner.)

From left to right, Johnny Ferrell (also known as Omar Bey), Harry Crafton, Pinkney Roberts, and Bill Hollis pose in their group the Atomic Senders around the 1950s. Bey started out performing on the *Parisian Tailors Colored Kiddies Hour* and went on to play in several groups throughout the northeast. (Courtesy of Diane Turner.)

Mickey Collins's band is pictured around the 1950s. The pool of jazz musicians dwindled during World War II as many went to fight in the war. Drummer Mickey Collins got his first real gig with Jimmy Adams and went on to form his own band. (Courtesy of Diane D. Turner.)

Mickey Collins is captured playing his drum in the 1940s. (Photograph by John W. Mosley, courtesy of Charles L. Blockson Afro-American Collection, Temple University Libraries.)

The *Parisian Tailors Kiddie Hour* was held on Sundays in the 1940s. Crowds would gather to support the youngsters and be entertained. Many musicians got their start performing there. In 1932, twelve-year-old Clarence Jackson signed a contract with WPEN and made his debut on *Parisian Tailors Colored Kiddies of the Air*. (Courtesy of Diane Turner.)

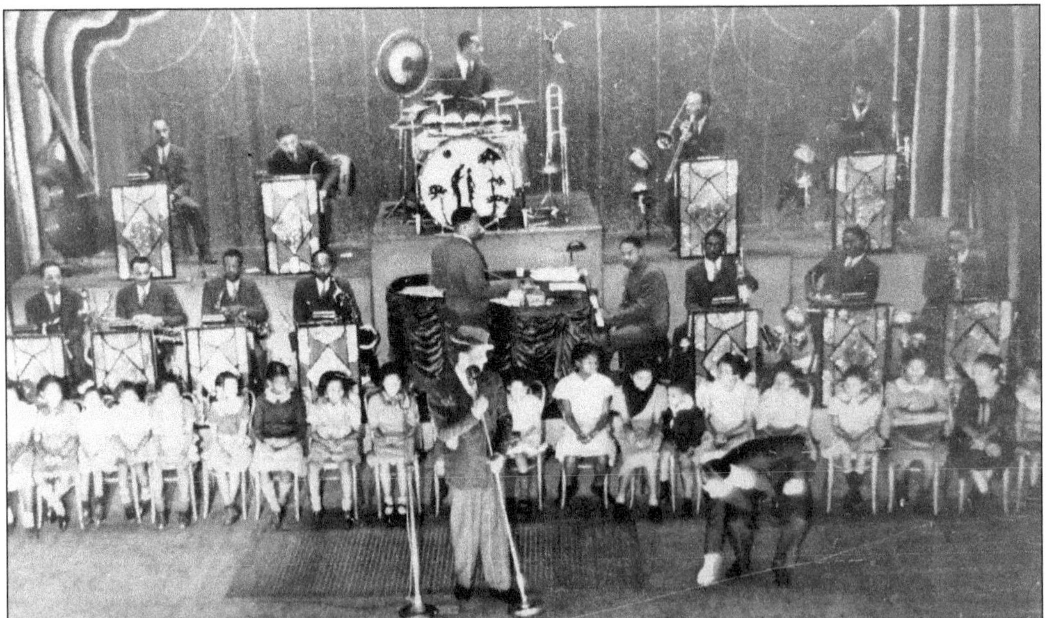

The Strand Ballroom, at Broad and Bainbridge Streets, was a lively place known as the "Cradle of Swing" during the 1930s. Promoter and songwriter Reese DuPree, who has been credited with composing "Shortnin' Bread," opened the Strand in 1933. He held weekly dances and performances with his house band, the Frankie Fairfax Orchestra. The Soaks Club presented Jimmy Gorham at the Strand Ballroom for a Saturday night dinner dance. (Photograph by John W. Mosley, courtesy of Charles L. Blockson Afro-American Collection, Temple University Libraries.)

The grand opening of the Battle of the Bands at the Strand Ballroom is pictured around the 1940s. Among the leaders of bands that participated in battles were Jimmy Gorham, Frankie Fairfax, C.S. Belton, and Smiling Billy Steward. (Courtesy of Cyd Mathis.)

Shown here is a 1944 advertisement of promoter Reese DuPree, who held weekly dances and performances at the Strand Ballroom. DuPree also held dances at O.V. Catto Auditorium, Town Hall, and Ambassador Hall. (Courtesy of Diane Turner.)

Duke Ellington (left) is pictured with promoter Reese DuPree (center) at the Pyramid Club around the 1950s. (Photograph by John W. Mosley, courtesy of Charles L. Blockson Afro-American Collection, Temple University Libraries.)

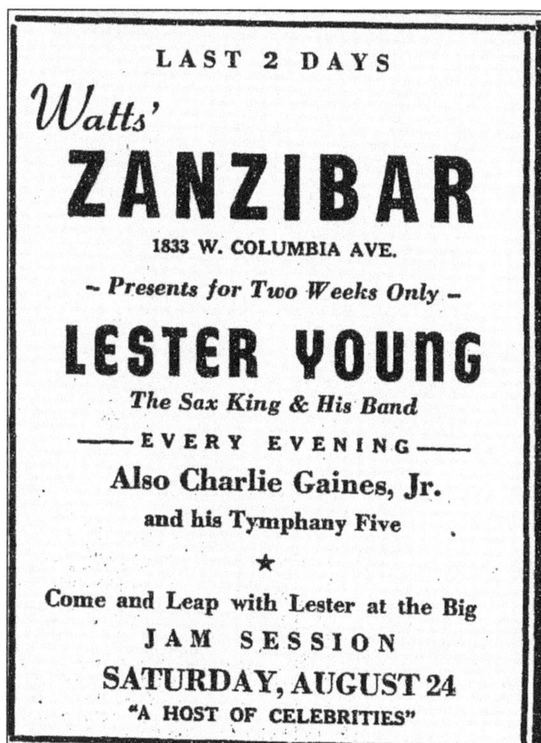

Robert and Richard Watt's Zanzibar club became known as the "bebop room" in Philly. It was the favorite hangout of most Philadelphia musicians who became legends, like John Coltrane, the Heath brothers, Philly Joe Jones, and Benny Golson. During August 1946, Lester Young performed at the club. Charlie Gaines Jr. led the house band. (Above, photograph by John W. Mosley, courtesy of Charles L. Blockson Afro-American Collection, Temple University Libraries; below, courtesy of the *Philadelphia Tribune*.)

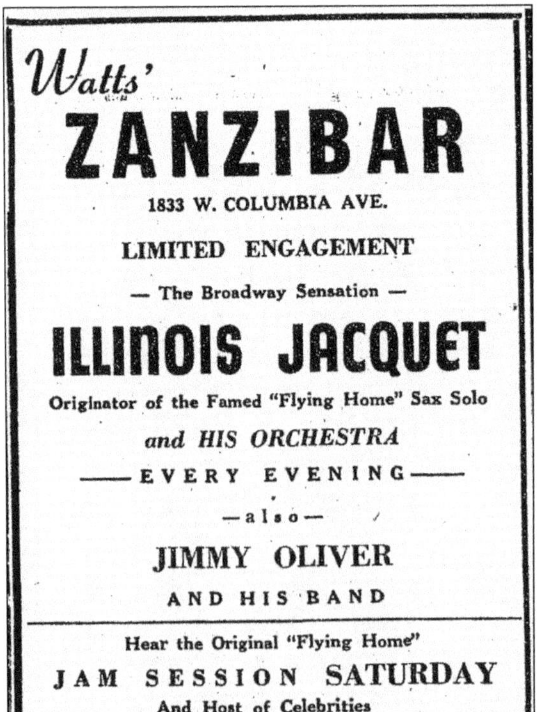

Clarinetist Illinois Jacquet is pictured at Watt's Zanzibar Club in September 1948. Then, tenor saxophonist Jimmy Oliver led the house band, consisting of bassist Percy Heath, drummer George "Butch" Ballard, and pianist Red Garland. Many people thought that Oliver's tone reminded them of Lester Young. (Above, courtesy of Charles L. Blockson Afro-American Collection, Temple University Libraries; below, courtesy of the *Philadelphia Tribune*)

Philadelphian Felix Valdera (at left holding paper and pen) owned two Paramount Records shops and was one of the most successful Black record store owners in the country. His stores, at 1519 South Street and 1801 Ridge Avenue, broke barriers in attracting an integrated clientele and advertised all over America. He had an hour-long show on WIBG radio called *Jumping at the Record Shop* and installed a recording studio in his store, which many record stores did at this time. The image below shows trumpeter Erskine Hawkins (right) making an appearance at the store. (Both photographs by John W. Mosley, courtesy of Charles L. Blockson Afro-American Collection, Temple University Libraries.)

Pictured here are Felix Valdera (second from left) and tenor saxophonist Illinois Jacquet (1922–2004) on the right. Valdera played host to more recording artists than any other Philadelphia record dealer. (Photograph by John W. Mosley, courtesy of Charles L. Blockson Afro-American Collection, Temple University Libraries.)

Shown here is the famous window display at the Paramount Records at 1519 South Street around the 1940s. (Photograph by John W. Mosley, courtesy of Charles L. Blockson Afro-American Collection, Temple University Libraries.)

The Nixon Grand Theatre presented Duke Ellington with songstress Ivy Anderson, captured in performance, on January 13, 1939. (Photograph by John W. Mosley, courtesy of Charles L. Blockson Afro-American Collection, Temple University Libraries.)

The Earle Theatre presented Duke Ellington in September 1945. Posing from left to right are Ellington with vocalists Kay Davis and Al Hibbler. (Photograph by John W. Mosley, courtesy of Charles L. Blockson Afro-American Collection, Temple University Libraries.)

The Benny Goodman Quartet included, from left to right, Teddy Wilson, Benny Goodman, and Lionel Hampton, pictured at the Earle Theatre on March 3, 1938. (Photograph by John W. Mosley, courtesy of Charles L. Blockson Afro-American Collection, Temple University Libraries.)

Pictured from left to right are Lionel Hampton, Benny Goodman, and Teddy Wilson. (Photograph by John W. Mosley, courtesy of Charles L. Blockson Afro-American Collection, Temple University Libraries.)

Shown here is a 1994 program from a jazz reunion celebrating Jewel's, which was located at 670 North Broad Street. It was known as "Philly's No. 1 Jazz Club" during the 1980s, when there was a new jazz explosion in Philadelphia. It was a place known to offer patrons delicious food and great jazz. (Courtesy of Charles L. Blockson Afro-American Collection, Temple University Libraries.)

Saxophonist, flutist, and composer Byard Lancaster performs with Dr. Donald Byrd at Jewel's in 1981. Musicians who were part of Jewel's stellar engagements included Al Grey, Betty Carter, Gloria Lynne, Jimmy Scott, Bill Doggett, Irene Reid, Don Patterson, Chico Hamilton, Pieces of a Dream, and others. (Courtesy of Diane D. Turner.)

Young baritone saxophonist, arranger, and composer Gerry Mulligan stands in front of WCAU as a member of the Elliot Lawrence Orchestra, the house band at the station. From his involvement in the *Birth of the Cool* recordings with Miles Davis to his legendary pianoless quartet in 1951 to the creation of the sound known as West Coast jazz, Mulligan played a vital role in the evolution of jazz. (Courtesy of the Library of Congress with permission from his widow Countess Franca Rota Borghini Baldovinetti.)

Elliot Lawrence, born Elliot Lawrence Broza, was the son of Stan Lee Broza and Esther Broza, radio and television pioneers who created the *Horn and Hardart Children's Hour* in Philadelphia, which ran on radio from 1927 to 1958. Lawrence became music director of the WCAU house band in 1945. In 1949, the band performed a three-week stint with the Nat King Cole Trio at the Paramount Theater in New York City, during which time it recorded Gerry Mulligan's tune "Elevation," later named "one of the top 50 best jazz recordings of the 20th century" by the Smithsonian. Later, Lawrence led the Tony Awards and composed film scores. It is important to note that, due to segregation and racism, there were no Black musicians in his early bands. (Courtesy of CBS Radio, 1946.)

Bassist Franklin Walker (left) is pictured with unidentified members of the O.V. Catto Orchestra, who performed at the O.V. Catto Club at Sixteenth and Fitzwater Streets in South Philadelphia under the management of Elks Lodge No. 20. In the downstairs grill, performances included musicians, tap dancers, comedians, and popular guest orchestras. The Elks lodge and club were named in honor of Octavius V. Catto (1839–1871), educator and activist. (Courtesy of Diane Turner.)

The Lincoln Theatre, at Broad and Lombard Streets, was a major venue for jazz. Patrons enjoyed performances by prominent jazz figures like Jimmy Lunceford, Cab Calloway, Duke Ellington, Louis Armstrong, and Tiny Bradshaw. It was also the home of *Parisian Tailors Colored Kiddie Hour* in the 1940s. (Photograph by John W. Mosley, courtesy of Charles L. Blockson Afro-American Collection, Temple University Libraries.)

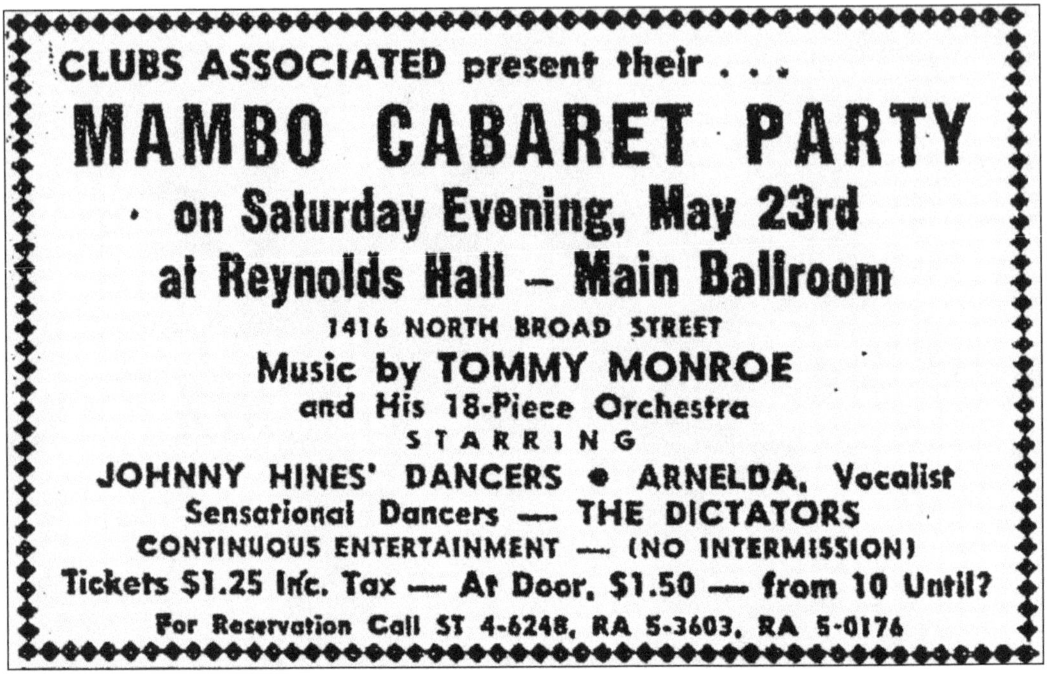

This is a 1953 ad for Tommy Monroe and His 18-Piece Orchestra. Bassist and promoter Tommy Monroe was a well-known local bandleader who studied at the Philadelphia Music Academy. He also became a promoter at the Tioga Theater at Seventeenth and Venango Streets, where Dizzy Gillespie, Lee Morgan, Jimmy Oliver, Don Gardner, and John Houston performed. Others whom Monroe brought to the theater included Felix Leach, Jimmy Stewart, Kenny Rogers, John Splawn, Sam Reed, Arthur Daniels, Tootie Heath, Jimmy Barnes, Sam Dockery, and Don Gardner. In the 1980s, Monroe opened T'N'T Monroe's at 1433 Arch Street with the house musicians consisting of Bootsie Barnes and His All-Star Band. (Courtesy of the *Philadelphia Tribune.*)

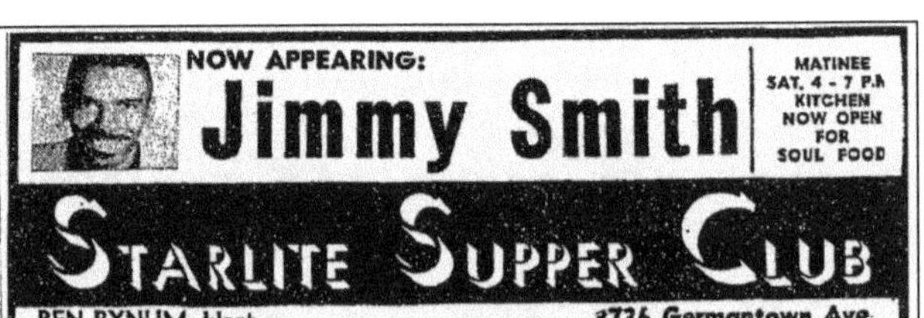

Benjamin "Ben" Bynum Sr. (1923–2021), a Montford Point Marine, businessman, nightclub, bar and restaurant owner, had a thriving Black business empire in Philadelphia. Bynum opened the Cadillac Club in North Philadelphia, where he became known for booking top acts like Count Basie, Woody Herman, Aretha Franklin, Nina Simone, and many others. Billy Paul's first album was *Feeling Good at The Cadillac Club.* Charlie Chisholm also recorded an album there. Pictured here are advertisements from his club, Starlite Supper Club, 3736 Germantown, featuring Willie Bobo (March 29, 1966) and Jimmy Smith (June 11, 1966). (Courtesy of the *Philadelphia Tribune.)*

Four

Woodshedding the Music

The Granoff School of Music was started in 1918 by Ukrainian violinist Isadore Granoff. After World War II, the school was approved to accept veterans' benefits, and musicians used the GI Bill to take courses. Unlike the esteemed Curtis Institute of Music, which was devoted entirely to the classical canon, Granoff taught just about every genre and produced many professional musicians in pop, big band, jazz, and Latin music. Bassist Percy Heath took some lessons there. Another notable student was saxophonist John Coltrane, mentored by Dennis Sandole, who developed his own unique teaching method and philosophy. Knowledge of complicated rhythmic, harmonic, and advanced melodic structures, Sandole felt, was necessary for his students to create and play an extraordinarily complex style of jazz. Some of Sandole's Philadelphia students included saxophonists Benny Golson, Billy Root, and Michael Brecker, jazz bagpiper and saxophonist Rufus Harley, and guitarist Pat Martino. Other noted musicians who studied at Granoff were trumpeter Dizzy Gillespie, saxophonist Sonny Fortune, and vocalist Billy Paul.

Avant-garde pianist and composer Leo Ornstein founded the Ornstein School of Music with his wife in Philadelphia at 1906 Spruce Street in the mid-1930s, and the school became busy with jazz musicians after the war. Organist Jimmy Smith was an alum, as were saxophonists John Coltrane and Bill Barron, but the school was sold by 1958. Many students switched to Combs College of Music, also in Center City, after the demise of Ornstein's school, and other jazz stars emerged like vibraphonist Khan Jamal and pianist Marc Copeland.

One cannot leave out one of Philly's most famous schools for turning out jazz stars: Mastbaum Vocational Technical High School. Trumpeter Lee Morgan auditioned for the dance band there in 1953, and within three years, Morgan was a member of the Dizzy Gillespie Orchestra. Other alumni included trumpeter Johnny Coles, drummer and trombonist Shep Shepard, trumpeter and bandleader Joe Wilder, trumpeter Red Rodney, clarinetist Buddy DeFranco, saxophonist Sam Reed, and clarinetist John LaPorta. This public high school was world famous for its music program, and the young students accepted into the program were considered well on their way to professional success.

Settlement Music School, founded in 1908, has branches all over the Philadelphia area and has some stellar jazz alumni, such as trumpeter Wallace Roney and violinist John Blake Jr.

The Granoff School of Music ran this advertisement for students on February 18, 1951. Founded by Isadore Granoff (1902–2000), a Ukrainian immigrant, at his rowhome at Eighth and Porter Streets in South Philadelphia, the school relocated to the Presser Building at Seventeenth and Chestnut Streets in 1928. Alumni of Granoff include Dizzy Gillespie, Sonny Fortune, and John Coltrane. Many of his students later became well-known classical, jazz, swing, big band and Latin musicians. (Courtesy of the *Philadelphia Inquirer*.)

Mastbaum Vocational Technical High School, at 3116 Frankford Avenue, was named for Jules E. Mastbaum, a civic-minded movie magnate and philanthropist. The school had one of the best music programs in the country for musicians playing big band swing and jazz. Some of its famous alumni include trumpeters Lee Morgan, Red Rodney, and Ted Curson. (Courtesy of Jules E. Mastbaum Alumni Association.)

Aside from the music schools and programs teaching popular music and jazz, the mentorship of new and up-and-coming musicians by professionals was a rich tradition and of prime importance in Philadelphia. Pianist Eddie Green (1933–2004) worked with Dexter Gordon, Pat Martino, Odeon Pope, Max Roach, Lou Rawls, and Jimmy Scott. He also recorded with female vocalists Rochelle Ferell, Suzanne Cloud, Etta James, and Miss Justine. Eddie Green performed at the Blue Note in the 1990s. (Photograph by Bruce Turner, courtesy of Charles L. Blockson Afro-American Collection, Temple University Libraries.)

William Nemoral "Sonny" Hoxter Jr. (1929–2021), pianist, bandleader, and composer, played in several local groups. He was a member of the jazz quintet The Philadelphians, which recorded two albums featuring Charlie Chisholm. He was also a member of the Perdidos Quintet and led his own bands. He worked at Freedom Theatre, where he composed music scores and performed on piano. Hoxter was a member with alto saxophonist Tony Williams of the Mount Airy Cultural Center, where he participated in youth workshops and provided music instruction. (Courtesy of Chere Shorter.)

Johnny Coles (1926–1997) performs at Penn's Landing in 1993. The trumpeter was nicknamed "Little Johnny C." After moving to Philly, he joined the group of first-class jazz musicians such as Benny Golson, Jimmy Heath, and John Coltrane. He spent his early career playing with R&B groups, including those of Eddie Vinson (1948–1951), Bull Moose Jackson (1952), and Earl Bostic (1955–1956). He was with James Moody from 1956 to 1958 and played with Gil Evans's orchestra between 1958 and 1964, including on the Miles Davis album *Sketches of Spain*. Coles recorded with Charles Mingus and his sextet, which also included Eric Dolphy, Clifford Jordan, Jaki Byard, and Dannie Richmond. Following this, he played with Herbie Hancock (1968–1969), Ray Charles (1969–1971), Duke Ellington (1971–1974), Art Blakey (1976), Dameronia, Mingus Dynasty, and the Count Basie Orchestra under the direction of Thad Jones (1985–1986). (Photograph by Bruce Turner, courtesy of Charles L. Blockson Afro-American Collection, Temple University Libraries.)

Morris "Mo" Bailey Jr. was a tenor saxophonist, composer, songwriter, producer, and arranger. He performed with Jimmy Smith, Bobby Timmons, McCoy Tyner, Ted Curson, Lee Morgan, Albert "Tootie" Heath, Spanky DeBrest, Reggie Workman, Art Farmer, Philly Joe Jones, Hassan Ibn Ali, Odean Pope, Richard "Groove" Holmes, and others. Focusing on arranging, recording and producing for 30 years, Bailey started playing tenor saxophone again in 1988 with jazz musicians like Sam Dockery, Lex Humphrey, Mickey Roker, Arthur Harper, and Bootsie Barnes. Bailey poses in Philadelphia around the 1980s. (Photograph by Millicent G. Muse, courtesy of Diane D. Turner.)

The Philadelphia Music Academy was founded in 1870 at 1617 Spruce Street in Philadelphia as a conservatory concentrating strictly on classical and symphonic music. Later, it would embrace musicians seeking popular and jazz instruction like bassist Stanley Clarke and saxophonist Michael Pedicin Jr. (Courtesy of Visual Resources and Special Collections, the University of the Arts.)

Dennis Sandole, born Dionigi Sandoli, was a jazz guitarist, composer, and music educator from Philadelphia. His older brother Adolph Sandole played sax, and the two began playing Philadelphia-area clubs during the 1930s, which led to him sharing the stage with such acts as Tommy Dorsey and Charlie Barnet. Moving to California, Sandole broke into session recording, appearing on numerous film soundtracks and records by Billie Holiday and Frank Sinatra, among others. As John Coltrane's mentor, Sandole taught advanced harmonic techniques that were applicable to any instrument, using exotic scales and creating his own. His students included saxophonists James Moody, Benny Golson, Michael Brecker, and Bobby Zankel; pianists Eric Spiegel and Sumi Tonooka; guitarists Jim Hall, Pat Martino, and Joe Federico; and Rufus Harley, the only jazz musician who played bagpipes. (Courtesy of FreshSounds Records.)

Gerald Price (1933–1996), pianist, composer, educator, and musical director, studied and played with Clifford Brown, Sarah Vaughn, Joe Williams, Sammy Davis Jr., Zoot Sims, and Sonny Stitt. He was Dakota Staton's longtime musical director and regularly performed at Zanzibar Blue and the Stratford Inn with singer Miss Justine. He not only mentored many young musicians, such as the group Pieces of a Dream, but also taught jazz theory and piano at Rowan University and Temple University. (Courtesy of Jim Holton.)

Saxophonists Larry McKenna (left) and Bootsie Barnes (right) perform. Larry McKenna, one of the most sought-out saxophone and jazz theory teachers in Philadelphia, has taught at the University of the Arts, Temple University Boyer College of Music, West Chester University, Widener University, and Community College of Philadelphia. He has played and recorded with Woody Herman, Clark Terry, Buddy DeFranco, Tony Bennett, Rosemary Clooney, and Frank Sinatra. (Photograph by Bruce Turner, courtesy of Charles L. Blockson Afro-American Collection, Temple University Libraries.)

Harrison Ridley (1938–2009), musicologist, WRTI Jazz host, and educator, was a central figure in jazz education. He taught at Temple University and Villanova University and gave presentations and workshops at the Philadelphia Clef Club and other institutions. From left to right, tenor saxophonist and educator Odeon Pope, Harrison Ridley, and bassist and educator Tyrone Brown pose at the Mellon Jazz Festival around the 1990s. (Photograph by Bruce Turner, courtesy of Charles L. Blockson Afro-American Collection, Temple University Libraries.)

Dizzy Gillespie (left) was known to be an influential yet informal educator. He was always ready to sit down at a piano and show another musician the elements of bebop or alternate chord voicings to bring out a different kind of melodic journey. In 1989, Gillespie was given the Grammy Lifetime Achievement Award. The next year, at the Kennedy Center for the Performing Arts ceremonies celebrating the centennial of American jazz, Gillespie received the Kennedy Center Honors Award and the American Society of Composers, Authors, and Publishers Duke Ellington Award for 50 years of achievement as a composer, performer, and bandleader. In 1989, Gillespie was awarded with an honorary doctorate of music from Berklee College of Music. Charles "Specs" Wright (right) got his name because it was said he could read undecipherable music manuscripts, just "specs" on a page. Wright was also known for teaching ear players how to read music. (Courtesy of Discogs.com.)

Shirley Scott (right), dubbed "Queen of the Organ," taught at Cheyney University of Pennsylvania. She recorded over 50 albums as a leader, mostly on the Prestige and Impulse labels. She performed regularly at Ortlieb's Jazzhaus and mentored young musicians like saxophonist Tim Warfield and trumpeter Terell Stafford (left). (Courtesy of Al Hunter Jr. of the *Philadelphia Daily News.*)

Pianist, organist, vocalist, and composer Trudy Pitts performs at Penn's Landing in the 1990s. Pitts was a noted mentor to many jazz musicians in Philadelphia, including noted pianist Orrin Evans. She recorded four albums for Prestige and taught at Temple University and at the University of the Arts. (Photograph by Bruce Turner, courtesy of Charles L. Blockson Afro-American Collection, Temple University Libraries.)

Five

Cutting Contests and Learning Lore

Dizzy Gillespie famously recalled that in the 1930s Philly had "some baaad jam sessions." These musical contests provided players opportunities to network and exchange musical ideas. Mothers of aspiring musicians such as the Heath brothers, Benny Golson, and McCoy Tyner played significant roles, offering spaces in their living rooms and even their places of business. Pianist McCoy Tyner held jam sessions with saxophonist Sam Reed, trumpeter Lee Morgan, and drummer Tootie Heath in his mother's beauty shop.

During the 1940s, Benny Golson and John Coltrane spent their Saturday afternoons hopping from one club to another on Columbia Avenue in North Philly competing with other young musicians. Young saxophonists Odean Pope and Morris "Mo" Bailey would start at one end of the strip and work their way down, listening outside and maybe stopping in each club along the way.

On Tuesday evenings in the mid-1950s, young jazz players would gather at Music City, a music store by day. Some came to listen, but many came to play in the weekly jams that co-owner and drummer Ellis Tollin ran above the store. Charlie Parker, Clifford Brown, Stan Getz, Sonny Stitt, and a host of stars would climb the stairs at Music City to play for hundreds of young fans, which often included such future innovators as Lee Morgan, Bobby Timmons, and Ted Curson.

Sessions popped up and disappeared quickly, but some popular ones became famous, like downstairs at the Douglass Hotel in the Rendezvous Lounge. The Black professionals playing the Earle Theatre and staying at the Douglass Hotel would sit in after the shows. Other longtime jams were at Budweiser Tavern, the Downbeat, Ridge Point, Durham's Casbah, the Club 200, Watt's Zanzibar, and Pep's. Local 274's union hall was also a popular proving ground for jazz musicians and fans to catch the best.

Later, the big draws featured the best rhythm sections. Pianist Eddie Green, bassist Tyrone Brown, and drummer Jim Miller held forth on Friday nights at Slim Cooper's; Monday nights at Lee Griffin's Blue Note, saxophonist Tony Williams hosted; saxophonist Bootsie Barnes and drummer Lex Humphries were at Natalie's; pianist Trudy Pitts and Mr. C sorted through the wannabes at Gert's; and Bob and Barbara's Lounge, a South Street staple since 1969, continues today. Pete Souders' Ortlieb's Jazzhaus, on Tuesday nights, had a legendary rhythm section featuring pianist Sid Simmons, bassist Mike Boone, and drummer Byron Landham. These men were the solid rock upon which many musicians found their musical footing or fell on their face.

Budweiser Tavern, at 1605 South Street, was known for good food, good drinks, and great entertainment. This draftee party was held on March 25, 1941. (Personal collection of Lillian Harris, courtesy of Diane Turner.)

Budweiser Tavern was a pioneer in jam sessions in 1940. On Monday and Thursday afternoons from 3:00 to 8:00 p.m., the place was always packed with patrons. (Personal collection of Lillian Harris, courtesy of Diane Turner.)

Lee Morgan performs on trumpet at Music City around 1956, when he was about 15 years old. Ellis Tollin's Music City, at 1033 Chestnut Street, was founded in 1947 as an instrument store. Eventually, Tollin transformed the fourth floor into a unique performance space where top jazz musicians, including Charlie Parker, Dizzy Gillespie, and Miles Davis, held jam sessions and mentored up-and-coming musicians like Lee Morgan, Bobby Timmons, and Archie Shepp on Tuesday nights. (Photograph by John W. Mosley, courtesy of Charles L. Blockson Afro-American Collection, Temple University Libraries.)

James Henry "Jimmy" Oliver (1924–2005), pictured in the center, a tenor saxophonist, migrated from Columbia, South Carolina, to North Philadelphia in 1925. He was in the house band at Watt's Zanzibar. He performed with Philly Joe Jones, Steve Davis, Red Garland, Dizzy Gillespie, Johnny Coles, Charlie Rice, Bootsie Barnes, the Heath brothers, and others. Drummer Mickey Roker is on the left with an unidentified person on the right. (Photograph by Pedro J. Matos, courtesy of the Charles L. Blockson Afro-American Collection.)

Cal Massey (1928–1972), trumpeter and composer, worked in the big bands of Jay McShann, Jimmy Heath, and Billie Holiday. In the 1950s, he led an ensemble with Jimmy Garrison, McCoy Tyner, and Tootie Heath. John Coltrane and Donald Byrd made guest performances. Massey became an activist, influenced by Malcolm X, involved in the Black Liberation, the Black Arts Movement, and affiliated with the Black Panther Party of the 1960s and 1970s. He believed in bringing his music to the people. Massey's compositions were recorded by John Coltrane, Lee Morgan, Jackie McLean, Philly Joe Jones, Freddie Hubbard, and Archie Shepp. He also performed with Romulus Franceschini in the Romas Orchestra. Pictured are Cal Massey and his daughter Waheeda backstage at Carnegie Hall, c. 1970s. (Courtesy of Zane Massey.)

Pictured from left to right are (first row) trumpeter Johnny Coles, tenor saxophonist James "Sax" Young, and bassist James "Sugie" Rhodes; (second row) Ray Bryant and John Coltrane at the Show Boat around the 1940s. (Courtesy of King Oliver.)

From left to right, tenor saxophonist Tony Williams, Scoop USA owner Sonny Driver, Pernell Council, tenor saxophonist Bootsie Barnes, club owner Dr. Chenet La Rose, and pianist Don Wilson pose at a Monday night jam session at Club La Rose around the 2000s. (Courtesy of Charles L. Blockson Afro-American Collection, Temple University Libraries.)

From left to right, tenor saxophonists Bootsie Barnes, Middy Middleton, Julian Pressley, Byard Lancaster, and Sam Reed jam at the African American Museum of Philadelphia during Presidential Jazz Week around the 1990s. (Photograph by Bruce Turner, courtesy of Charles L. Blockson Afro-American Collection, Temple University Libraries.)

From left to right tenor are saxophonist Bootsie Barnes and guitarist George Benson with bassist Arthur Harper in the background at Ortlieb's Jazzhaus at a Wednesday night session around the 1990s. (Photograph by Pedro J. Matos, courtesy of the Charles L. Blockson Afro-American Collection, Temple University Libraries.)

At the Philadelphia Clef Club inside the union building, service was provided to patrons by, from left to right, doorman Billy Williams, barmaid Lillian Harris, Pres. Jimmy Adams, barmaid Bert Pressley, and hostess Georgia Keeys. (Courtesy of Diane D. Turner.)

Pictured from left to right in a promotional photograph for the Al Stauffer Trio are drummer Jim Miller, bassist Al Stauffer, and pianist Tom Lawton sometime in the 1980s. Miller, a longtime educator at Rowan University, was also founder and president of Dreambox Media, a Philadelphia jazz record label documenting the music from 1986 to 2015. Stauffer was a revered jazz theory teacher with an office in South Philly. Lawton is on the jazz faculty at Temple University and the University of the Arts and plays regularly with saxophonist Odean Pope. Lawton told *All About Jazz* regarding Stauffer, "in addition to being a great bassist, he taught improvisation to musicians of all instruments in Philadelphia. I can think of maybe ten or twenty players in Philly who studied improv with him . . . he showed me things that happened in a million tunes, and it made learning all the tunes much easier than having to learn each tune as a brand-new thing." (Photograph by Candice DiCarlo and Courtesy of Tom Lawton.)

Shown from left to right are WRTI-FM radio personality and historian Harrison Ridley, bagpipe player Rufus Harley, and radio personality Reggie Bryant at the Philadelphia Clef Club for a jam session fundraiser for vibraphonist Khan Jamal around the 2000s. Bryant and journalist and newscaster Brahin Ahmaddiya (1942–2000) were strong supporters and promoters of jazz. (Courtesy of Charles L. Blockson Afro-American Collection, Temple University Libraries.)

Tenor saxophonist Jimmy Oliver (left) and bassist Arthur Harper (right) jam at Ortlieb's Jazzhaus around the 1990s. (Photograph by Pedro Matos, courtesy of Charles L. Blockson Afro-American Collection, Temple University Libraries.)

Tenor saxophonist Sam Reed and bassist Lee Smith jam at Chris' Jazz Cafe in the 1990s. (Photograph by Bruce Turner, courtesy of Charles L. Blockson Afro-American Collection, Temple University Libraries.)

Six

Philly Legends and Mainstays

Philadelphia, always a cradle of jazz, nurtured, developed, and celebrated jazz musicians and singers. From early on, the city exploded with stars like Ethel Waters, a nightclub, stage, and movie star; Bessie Smith, the "Empress of the Blues," who moved to Philly in 1922 and lived on Christian Street; Billie Holiday, who was born here and played the top nightclubs in the city and the famed Earle Theater throughout her life; and Pearl Bailey, who saxophonist Bootsie Barnes said used to push him around in his baby carriage. Other legends include Dizzy Gillespie, John Coltrane, Benny Golson, McCoy Tyner, Shirley Scott, Nina Simone, Charlie Ventura, Jimmy Smith, Bill Doggett, Buddy DeFranco, Sun Ra, Philly Joe Jones, Johnny Coles, Gerry Mulligan, Lee Morgan, Red Rodney, Joe Wilder, the Heath brothers, Trudy Pitts, Odean Pope, and Grover Washington Jr. They became legends because they were serious and dedicated to the music. They grew up listening all day, especially because jazz was the popular music. It was everywhere—on the radio and Victrola record players, in clubs, on neighborhood streets, at dances, in theaters, and at social events. Shirley Scott listened to live music in her home. Her brother played saxophone, and his friends included Red Garland, Fats Wright, and Philly Joe Jones, who lived in their North Philadelphia neighborhood and rehearsed at their house. She paid attention to Garland and Wright, who not only influenced her but instructed her. By the time Scott was in the 12th grade, she was accomplished enough to go on the road with drummer James "Coatesville" Harris's band.

Young lions such as John Coltrane, Benny Golson, Percy Heath, and Lee Morgan spent many hours, both day and night, learning, studying, practicing, and rehearsing. Percy Heath's mother was his main supporter. He recalled, "I remember the first two, three years we always had a set of drums in the middle of the living room floor, it was just a mess. She put up with it." Most of all, these Philly legends were fortunate to reside in a city with great promoters, excellent schools, and lots of music venues. Young musicians were encouraged to enter the entertainment field, garnering early recognition by competing in weekly amateur shows. Renowned jazz musicians came to Philly to perform and were accessible to aspiring jazz musicians, and there were veteran jazz musicians residing in the city who mentored young jazz lions.

Billie Holiday (1915–1959), jazz vocalist and songwriter, was born Eleanora Fagan at Philadelphia General Hospital at Thirty-Fourth and Pine Streets. Her influences included Bessie Smith and Louis Armstrong. She reinvented modern singing and performance conventions. Lester Young affectionately named her "Lady Day." She recorded and performed with Benny Goodman, Lester Young, Count Basie, Artie Shaw, and others. Holiday's signature song became "Strange Fruit," a civil rights protest song depicting lynching. Billie Holiday meets a sergeant at the South Broad Street USO after a performance in 1943. (Photograph by John W. Mosley, courtesy of Charles L. Blockson Afro-American Collection, Temple University Libraries.)

Billie Holiday frequently performed in Philly at venues like the Academy of Music and various clubs such as the Cheeko Club (8100 Roosevelt Boulevard), Ebony Club (Broad and Spruce Streets), the Show Boat (1409 Lombard Street), Fays (Fortieth and Market Streets), and Pep's Musical Bar. Billie Holiday and Roy Eldridge are pictured after finishing an all-star jazz concert at Town Hall in May 1946. (Photograph by John W. Mosley, courtesy of Charles L. Blockson Afro-American Collection, Temple University Libraries.)

Pearl Mae Bailey (1918–1990), singer and actress, started her career singing and dancing in nightclubs in Philly during the 1930s. She made her Broadway debut in *St. Louis Woman* in 1946. In 1968, she won a Tony Award for the title role in the all-Black production of *Hello, Dolly!* In 1970, she was appointed "Ambassador of Love" by Pres. Richard Nixon. In 1987, Bailey won a Daytime Emmy Award for her performance as a fairy godmother in *Cindy Eller: A Modern Fairy Tale* on ABC. She sent this signed promotional portrait to bassist John Ferrell. (Courtesy of Diane D. Turner.)

Ethel Waters (1896–1977), singer and actress, was one of the best-known artists of her time. She sang jazz, blues, gospel, and popular music genres. She starred in her own television show, *Beulah*. In 1961, she earned an Emmy Award for her performance in the television series *Route 66*. She performed on Broadway and had leading roles in Hollywood films, where she earned an Academy Award nomination in the film *Pinky*. She is pictured in 1938. (Courtesy of the William Gottlieb Collection, Library of Congress.)

Shirley Scott (1934–2002), pianist, organist, composer and educator, was known as the "Queen of the Organ." She was influenced by pianists such as Red Garland and Fats Wright, who took the time to teach her. When she was in the twelfth grade, she went on the road with Coatesville Harris's band. During the 1950s, Scott played with saxophonist Eddie "Lockjaw" Davis. She also performed with her husband, Stanley Turrentine. During the 1970s, Scott led her own band. Scott performs at the African American Museum in Philadelphia around the 1990s. (Photograph by Jack T. Franklin, courtesy of African American Museum in Philadelphia.)

Pictured at Temple University around the 1990s are, from left to right, (first row) Sue Ford, Shirley Scott, and Don Gardner; (second row) Bootsie Barnes and Danny Turner. (Photograph by Bruce Turner, courtesy of Charles L. Blockson Afro-American Collection, Temple University Libraries.)

William Ballard "Bill" Doggett (1916–1996), jazz and R&B pianist, organist, and arranger, was the music director for the Frankie Fairfax Orchestra before starting his own band. He is best known for his composition recorded in 1956, "Honky Tonk." He worked and arranged with the Ink Spots, Louis Jordan, Ella Fitzgerald, Lionel Hampton, Louis Armstrong, and Count Basie. Doggett gave Dizzy Gillespie his nickname when Gillespie auditioned for the Frankie Fairfax band very early in his career. Doggett is pictured in May 1956. (Courtesy of Charles L. Blockson Afro-American Collection, Temple University Libraries.)

John Birks "Dizzy" Gillespie (1917–1993), trumpeter, bandleader, composer, singer, and educator, was a major architect of bebop known for incorporating Afro-Cuban rhythms and other ethnic elements in his music. He gained recognition in the Frankie Fairfax Orchestra. He was hired by Teddy Hill, moved to New York City, and continued to experiment with new ideas and concepts. He performed in big bands and with musicians like Cab Calloway, Earl "Fatha" Hines, Billy Eckstine, Gene Ammons, Yusef Lateef, Paul Gonsalves, Jimmy Heath, James Moody, Ray Bryant, Kenny Clarke, John Coltrane, and others. Gillespie befriended Charlie Parker and recorded with him in 1945. He also served as a jazz ambassador for the State Department. Here Gillespie performs on congas in 1975 at Abron Arts Center, Henry Street Settlement House, in New York City. (Photograph by Bill May, courtesy of Charles L. Blockson Afro-American Collection, Temple University Libraries.)

Beryl Booker (1922–1978) was a jazz pianist and composer who played with the Slam Stewart Trio in 1946. She also accompanied Dinah Washington. In 1952, she formed a quintet and played at Birdland, and in 1953, she formed a trio of women that toured Europe. Booker recorded as a leader for Victor. Here, Lionel Hampton and Beryl Booker perform together around the 1950s. (Photograph by John W. Mosley, courtesy of Charles L. Blockson Afro-American Collection, Temple University Libraries.)

From left to right, bebop vocalist, self-published author and poet Babs Gonzales (1919–1980); trumpeter and bandleader Red Rodney (1927–1994); trumpeter, composer, and bandleader Dizzy Gillespie (1917–1993); and tenor saxophonist and bandleader Charlie Ventura (1916–1992) are pictured around the 1940s. (Photograph by John W. Mosley, courtesy of Charles L. Blockson Afro-American Collection, Temple University Libraries.)

Robert "Red Rodney" Chudnick worked in big bands at an early age. He appeared with Jimmy Dorsey, Georgie Auld, Claude Thornhill, Gene Krupa, Benny Goodman, Wood Herman, and others. He was first influenced by Harry James and later played with bebop trumpeter Howard McGhee. He met Charlie Parker in 1944 and was offered a trumpet chair with his quintet in 1949. (Courtesy of William Gottlieb Collection, Library of Congress.)

Charles "Charlie" Ventura (1916–1992), tenor saxophonist and bandleader, started playing on C-melody sax. He switched to alto and then to tenor. In 1942, he joined Gene Krupa's big band. In 1945, he won a *Down Beat* magazine award as Krupa's featured soloist. In 1946, Ventura formed and led his own big band. Ventura sent this c. 1940s signed promotional photograph to his friend drummer Butch Ballard. (Courtesy of Mr. and Mrs. Michael Green.)

From left to right, pianist Beryl Booker, singer "Bon Bon" Tunnell, tenor saxophonist Earl Bostic (1913–1965), and record store owner and producer Felix Valdera are pictured around the 1940s. (Photograph by John W. Mosley, courtesy of Charles L. Blockson Afro-American Collection, Temple University Libraries.)

Nina Simone (1933–2003), born Eunice Kathleen Waymon, was an American singer, songwriter, pianist, arranger, and civil rights activist widely associated with jazz music. Simone aspired to become a classical pianist while working in a broad range of styles including classical, jazz, blues, folk, R&B, gospel, and popular. Simone applied to Curtis Institute of Music in Philadelphia but was denied admission because of her color. She went on to study at Juilliard in New York City. During her career, she referred to her music as Black Classical Music. She is pictured around the 1960s. (Photograph by Jack T. Franklin, courtesy of the African American Museum of Philadelphia.)

Drummer Charlie Rice (1920–2018) was an anchor of the Philly jazz scene in the 1940s and 1950s as a member of the Downbeat Club house band. During Rice's career, he played with Dizzy Gillespie, John Coltrane, Red Garland, Jimmy Heath, Benny Golson, Chet Baker, Shirley Scott, Louis Jordan, and many others. The Charlie Rice Quartet included tenor saxophonist Tim Warfield, pianist Don Wilson, and bassist Lee Smith in 2007. From left to right are James "Jimmy" Morgan, brother of Lee Morgan, drummer Max Roach, and drummer Charlie Rice backstage at a concert held at Penn's Landing in the 1990s. (Photograph by Bruce Turner, courtesy of Charles L. Blockson Afro-American Collection, Temple University Libraries.)

Drummer George Edward "Butch" Ballard (1918–2011) was taught early on by Professor Coles, bandmaster of the O.V. Catto Elks of Philadelphia. His first performance was at the Frankford Boys Club. His first professional gig was with Louis Armstrong's band. He played with many great jazz artists like Cootie Williams, Count Basie, Pearl Bailey, Clark Terry, Shirley Scott, Bootsie Barnes, Ella Fitzgerald, and Eddie "Lockjaw" Davis. Butch Ballard stands at left with drum in his hand around the 1930s (Courtesy of Diane D. Turner.)

Joe Wilder (1922–2014) trumpeter, composer, and bandleader, was born into a musical family. His father, Curtis Wilder (1900–2001), was a bassist and bandleader. Wilder's first performances were aired on *Parisian Tailors Colored Kiddies Hour*. A Montford Point Marine, Wilder was one of the first Blacks to serve in the US Marines during World War II. He played with Jimmie Lunceford, Noble Sissle, Dizzy Gillespie, Count Basie, Cab Calloway, Louis Armstrong, and others. He was a regular sideman and favorite of Gil Evans, Hank Jones, Benny Goodman, Billie Holiday, Lena Horne, Harry Belafonte, Tony Bennett, and Johnny Mathis. Wilder's awards include a Temple University Jazz Master's Hall of Fame Award in 2006 and the National Endowment for the Arts Jazz Masters Award in 2008. Wilder performs at the Jazz Room at William Patterson University in Wayne, New Jersey, around the 1980s. (Photograph by Bill May, courtesy of Charles L. Blockson Afro-American Collection, Temple University Libraries.)

James "Jimmy" Hamilton (1917–1994), clarinetist, tenor saxophonist, and bandleader, grew up in Philadelphia and played in local bands with Bill Doggett, Teddy Wilson, Lucky Millinder, and others. Hamilton was a member of the Duke Ellington Orchestra from 1943 to 1968. He recorded as a leader and sideman with Duke Ellington, Johnny Hodges, Lucky Thompson, Ben Webster, Coleman Hawkins, Earl Hines, and others. Jimmy Hamilton poses around the 1940s. (Photograph by John W. Mosley, courtesy of Charles L. Blockson Afro-American Collection, Temple University Libraries.)

Philadelphia native William Osborne "Billy" Kyle (1914–1966), pianist and composer, played with Lucky Millinder, John Kirkby's sextet, Sy Oliver, Tiny Bradshaw, and others. He became a member of Louis Armstrong's All-Stars. He recorded as a leader and sideman with Louis Armstrong, Ella Fitzgerald, Charlie Shavers, Rex Stewart, Buck Clayton, Al Hibbler, and Dave Brubeck. He coauthored "Billy's Bounce." His album *Finishing Up a Date* was released in 1988. (Courtesy of Charles L. Blockson Afro-American Collection, Temple University Libraries.)

James Raleigh "Jymie" Merritt (1926–2020), bassist, composer, and bandleader, was a pioneer of the electric bass who started out with the tenor saxophone. He grew up in Philadelphia playing with Benny Golson and Philly Joe Jones. He received training on the upright bass at the Ornstein School of Music with Philadelphia Orchestra bassist Carl Torello. In 1940, he toured with Bull Moose Jackson, and he joined Art Blakey in 1958. Merritt appeared on 18 albums with Art Blakey and the Jazz Messengers. He worked with Lee Morgan, Dizzy Gillespie, Max Roach, and Chet Baker. (Photograph by Bruce Turner, courtesy of Charles L. Blockson Afro-American Collection, Temple University Libraries.)

James W. "Coatesville" (or "Coats") Harris (1918–1970), drummer and bandleader, earned a reputation as an exceptional musician. He played with Jimmy Shorter and Jimmy Gorham during the 1940s and joined Local 274 in 1935. He made it big when he toured with Louis Armstrong. He formed his own group, Coatesville Harris and his Fabulous Six, and led the house band at Spider Kelly's on Mole Street in Philadelphia and other East Coast venues. He is seen in this c. 1950s candid shot. (Photograph by John W. Mosley, courtesy of Charles L. Blockson Afro-American Collection, Temple University Libraries.)

Rufus Harley Jr. (1936–2006), a native of Philadelphia, was referred to as the International Ambassador Messenger of Music, Culture, and Freedom. He was known primarily as the world's first and only jazz bagpipe virtuoso in addition to being an international ambassador for peace. In 1965, Harley released his first album performing on bagpipes titled, *Bagpipe Blues*. (Courtesy of photographer L. David Hinton.)

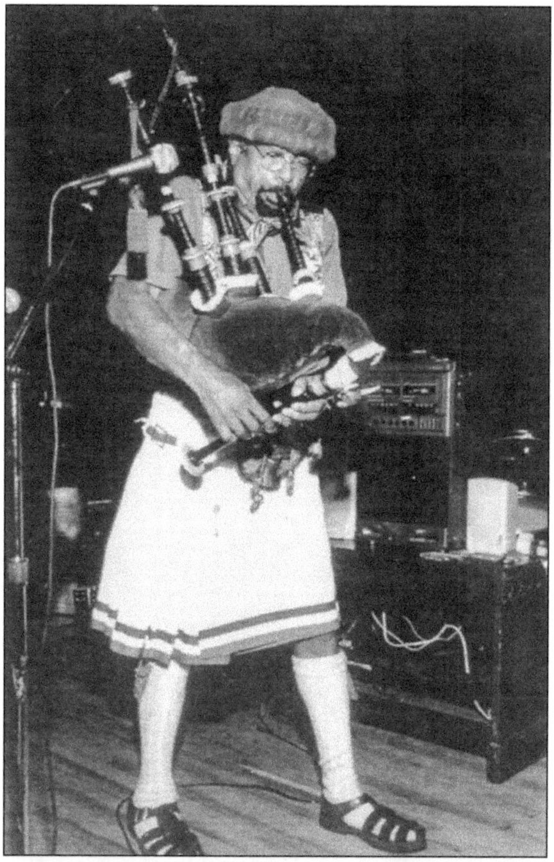

Saxophonist Jimmy Oliver (center) performs with bassist Stanley Clarke (left) and drummer Mickey Roker (right) at the Mellon Jazz Festival around the 1990s. (Photograph by Pedro J. Matos, courtesy of Diane D. Turner.)

Pianist Kenny Gates, trumpeter Johnny Coles, and comedian Tommy "Red Fox" Jordan are pictured (left to right) at Lex Humphries's memorial service in the 1990s. (Photograph by Bruce Turner, courtesy of Charles L. Blockson Afro-American Collection, Temple University Libraries.)

Bill Carney's Hi Tones, pictured around 1952–1953, are, from left to right, (seated) Albert "Tootie" Heath, Shirley Scott, and John Coltrane; (standing) and Bill "Mr. C" Carney. William Theodore Carney Jr. (1925–2017), or Mr. C, a Montford Point Marine, became a well-known drummer, jazz band leader, and an acclaimed promoter of jazz in Philadelphia working with his wife Trudy Pitts, Pat Martino, Ben Webster, George Benson, Sonny Stitt, Gene Ammons, the Philadelphia Clef Club, and many others. (Photograph by Jack T. Franklin, courtesy of African American Museum of Philadelphia.)

Bassist Arthur Harper (1939–2004) worked with Jimmy Heath, Wes Montgomery, Ray Bryant, Shirley Scott, J.J. Johnson, Bud Powell, Mary Lou Williams, Betty Carter, and others. Harper performed regularly at Ortlieb's Jazzhaus. Here he performs during the Mellon Jazz Festival at Penn's Landing in the 1990s. (Photograph by Bruce Turner, courtesy of Charles L. Blockson Afro-American Collection, Temple University Libraries.)

Tenor saxophonist Myrtle Young (1923–2010) received her early musical training at Piney Woods Country Life School, where she joined the all-girl school band, which later became the International Sweethearts of Rhythm. They performed until 1948 under the direction of Prof. Laurence C. Jones. Young settled in Philadelphia and organized Myrtle Young and Her Rays of Rhythm. She appeared on many gigs with Bootsie Barnes, Shirley Scott, Dottie Smith, Toni Rose, and Pearl Williams. Myrtle Young is pictured holding her saxophone around the 1950s. (Courtesy of Charles L. Blockson Afro-American Collection, Temple University Libraries.)

Grover Washington Jr. (1943–1999) was a jazz-funk/soul-jazz saxophonist and composer. Considered by many to be one of the founders of the smooth jazz genre, Washington later became an arranger and producer. Pictured here is Grover Washington Jr. performing at the Panasonic Headquarters in Secaucus, New Jersey, on August 12, 1993. (Photograph by Bill May, courtesy of Charles L. Blockson Afro-American Collection, Temple University Libraries.)

Sid Simmons (1946–2010), pianist and composer, started his career in the Visitors with Carl and Earl Grubbs. He joined and recorded with Grover Washington Jr. He also worked and recorded with Philly Joe Jones, John Blake, Norman Connors, Valery Ponomorev, Billy Pierce, Gary Bartz, Bootsie Barnes, John Swana, Joe Magnarelli, Mike Boone, Byron Landham, and others. He was in the Ortlieb's Jazzhaus house band and a frequent sideman at Zanzibar Blue, Candlelight Lounge, Chris's Jazz Café, and others. Tenor and soprano saxophonist Tim Warfield and Sid Simmons perform at Millcreek Recreational Center around the 1990s. (Photograph by Bruce Turner, courtesy of Charles L. Blockson Afro-American Collection, Temple University Libraries.)

From left to right, drummer Jonathan Blake (son), bassist Mike Boone, violinist John Blake Jr. (father), and pianist Sid Simmons perform at the Philadelphia Clef Club in the 1990s. (Photograph by Bruce Turner, courtesy of Charles L. Blockson Afro-American Collection, Temple University Libraries.)

Drummer Millard "Pete" Vinson (1949–2008) played in the Sam Reed Orchestra at the Uptown Theatre. He toured and recorded with Grover Washington Jr. He also worked with Johnny Hartman, Little Jimmy Scott, Rachelle Ferrell, and Johnny Coles. He was a member of the trio Fortune Vinson Cruse. (Photograph by Bruce Turner, courtesy of Charles L. Blockson Afro-American Collection, Temple University Libraries.)

Pictured from left to right are trumpeter John Swana, trombonist Clifford Adams, and tenor saxophonist Bootsie Barnes at the Millcreek Recreational Center in the 1990s. (Photograph by Bruce Turner, courtesy of Charles L. Blockson Afro-American Collection, Temple University Libraries.)

Pictured from left to right are drummer Byron Landham, bassist Russell Malone, tenor saxophonist Bootsie Barnes, and organist "Papa John" DeFrancesco in the 1990s. (Photograph by Bruce Turner, courtesy of Charles L. Blockson Afro-American Collection, Temple University Libraries.)

Granville "Mickey" Roker Jr. started playing drums at Bartlett Junior High and in the Bugle & Drums Corps at the Octavius V. Catto Elks at Sixteenth and Fitzwater Streets. Jam sessions were held everywhere including his home with Arthur Harper, Reggie Workman, McCoy Tyner, Kenny Barron, Calvin Ector, Eddie Campbell, Dave Jackson, Lee Morgan, C-Sharp, and Leon Grimes. He started out gigging with R&B groups like King James, Jimmy Devine, and Fred Bullock. He was inspired by drummers Al Jones, Specs Wright, and Eddie Campbell. Moving to jazz, he played with Sam Reed, Jimmy Oliver, Odean Pope, Jimmy Heath, Johnny Coles, Danny Turner, and others. In 1959, Reggie Workman called him, and he played with GiGi Gryce, then in a trio with Arthur Harper and Ray Bryant. He has performed with Ron Carter, Bobby Timmons, Bob Cranshaw, and Mary Lou Williams. He has also played and recorded with Duke Pearson, Stanley Turrentine, Shirley Scott, Frank Foster, Nancy Wilson, Sonny Rollins, Milt Jackson, Lee Morgan, Dizzy Gillespie, Ray Brown, and Ella Fitzgerald. He is pictured around the 1990s. (Photograph by Bruce Turner, courtesy of Charles L. Blockson Afro-American Collection, Temple University Libraries.)

Lex P. Humphries III (1936–1994) graduated from Mastbaum Vocational Technical High School. He played in high school bands with Spanky DeBrest, Ernie Duncan, Tootie Heath, Bootsie Barnes, and Lee Morgan. He became a sought-after drummer who played, traveled, performed, and recorded with jazz greats like John Coltrane, Dizzy Gillespie, Hank Mobley, Donald Byrd, Yusef Lateef, Freddie Hubbard, Lester Young, Benny Golson, McCoy Tyner, Curtis Fuller, Bill Evans, Slide Hampton, Paul Chambers, Art Farmer, Sun Ra, and others. (Courtesy of Diane D. Turner.)

Drummer Robert Joseph "Bobby" Durham (1937–2008) played with Duke Ellington, Lionel Hampton, Oscar Peterson, and Ella Fitzgerald. From 1966 to 1971, he formed a trio with pianist Oscar Peterson and bassist Ray Brown. He recorded with trumpeters Dizzy Gillespie and Roy Eldridge, pianist Tommy Flanagan, guitarist Joe Pass, and alto saxophonist Benny Carter. (Photograph by Bruce Turner, courtesy of Charles L. Blockson Afro-American Collection, Temple University Libraries.)

Drummer Edgar Bateman (1929–2010) performed at the Philadelphia Clef Club, where he coached and gave clinics and workshops; he also gave masterclasses at Temple University. He played at Zanzibar Blue, the Philadelphia Ethnical Society, the African American Museum of Philadelphia, the Painted Bride Art Center, and other venues and festivals. He performed or recorded with Eric Dolphy, Herbie Hancock, Booker Ervin, Walt Dickerson, Khan Jamal, and others. Bateman is pictured in 1994. (Photograph by Bruce Turner, courtesy of Charles L. Blockson Afro-American Collection, Temple University Libraries.)

James Andrew "Hicks" Glenn (1937–2000), bassist and cofounder of the Mill Creek Jazz and Cultural Society, played with Clifford Jordan, David "Fathead" Newman, and Philly Joe Jones. He was a member of the Philadelphia Jazz All-Stars with Bootsie Barnes and Sid Simmons. Glenn is pictured with drummer Craig McIver at Millcreek Recreational Center in the 1990s. (Photograph by Bruce Turner, courtesy of Charles L. Blockson Afro-American Collection, Temple University Libraries.)

Charles Earland (1941–1999), an internationally known jazz organist, began his career playing tenor saxophone with the Temple University Band and then joined Jimmy McGriff's band. In 1963, he switched to organ. Earland recorded with Lou Donaldson, Stanley Turrentine, Grover Washington Jr., Freddie Hubbard, Art Blakey, and Joe Henderson. Earland performs at Zanzibar Club in the 1990s. (Photograph by Bruce Turner, courtesy of Charles L. Blockson Afro-American Collection, Temple University Libraries.)

James H. "Jimmy" McGriff (1936–2008), who was a master on the Hammond B-3 organ known for his soulful sound, studied at Juilliard School, Combs College of Music, and Temple University. He played with Ray Charles and collaborated with Hank Crawford, Bernard "Pretty" Purdie, and Junior Parker. He also performed with Wynton Marsalis, Count Basie, Buddy Rich, and Dizzy Gillespie. Jimmy McGriff performs at Penn's Landing in the 1990s. (Photograph by Bruce Turner, courtesy of Charles L. Blockson Afro-American Collection, Temple University Libraries.)

Tenor saxophonist Samuel "Sam" Reed (1935–2021) performed with jazz icon Billie Holiday at the Cheeko Club. He was leader of the house band at the Uptown Theatre, where he hired local musicians to back jazz and R&B artists such as Patti LaBelle, Diana Ross and the Supremes, and others. He toured with Teddy Pendergrass. His quartet teamed up with international singer Denise King. Reed performed regularly at the Philadelphia Clef Club and the Top Shelf Lounge. He is pictured here in the 1990s with bassist Lee Smith. (Photograph by Bruce Turner, courtesy of Charles L. Blockson Afro-American Collection, Temple University Libraries.)

Billy James (1936–2009) began playing percussion at 15 years old with the Lionel Hampton Orchestra. He toured and recorded with Don Patterson, Pat Martino, Gene Ammons, Sonny Stitt, Zoot Sims, Eddie "Lockjaw" Davis, Booker Ervin, David "Fathead" Newman, Etta Jones, Houston Person, and Carmen McRae. He performed with Bootsie Barnes, Eddie Harris, Clark Terry, Mose Allison, Wynton Kelly, Milton Hinton, and others. He was a mainstay at Ortlieb's Jazzhaus and Chris' Jazz Café. (Courtesy of Diane D. Turner.)

John Nathaniel "Nate" Murray (1937–2021) bassist, bandleader, and promoter, was known as the ambassador of the Philadelphia music scene. He provided clubs with entertainers like Sonny Fortune, George Barron, Any Aaron, Carl Holmes, Bobby Eli, Walter Miller, Alfie Pollitt, Earl Jones, the fusion group Reverie, Cliff Edwards, Umar Raheem, the Budessa brothers, Leroy Hawkes, and others. Former director of the African American Museum of Philadelphia Terri Doke (left) and Murray (right) are pictured at a Jazz People's Collective event at Rhythm's Club in the 1990s. (Patented Photos, courtesy of Diane D. Turner.)

Leonard "Doc" Gibbs (1948–2021), a percussionist and bandleader raised in West Philadelphia, was a member of Grover Washington Jr.'s band. He toured with many jazz, R&B, and soul artists, including George Benson, Nany Wilson, Al Jarreau, Bob James, and Erykah Badu. He was musical director and bandleader for Emeril Lagasse's Food Network show. (Photograph by Bruce Turner, courtesy of Charles L. Blockson Afro-American Collection, Temple University Libraries.)

Charles Bowen Sr. is pictured at the Foxhole on Locust Walk in Philadelphia in 1977. Tenor saxophonist Bowen performed with many Philly greats and was an important mentor to Nasir Dickerson, Shirley Scott, Sunny Murray, Philly Joe Jones, Butch Ballard, Sonny Hoxter, James "Hicks" Glenn, Eddie Green, Charles Fambrough, and others. (Courtesy of photographer H. Alonzo Jennings.)

Charlie Chisholm, trumpeter, flugelhorn player, bandleader, jazz historian, and jazz promoter, attended the Edith Landis Musical Institute at Seventeenth and Market Streets. While attending Ben Franklin High School, he befriended Benny Golson, and they formed a jazz band. They gigged with John Coltrane. He was a member of The Philadelphians and pioneered bebop with Charlie Parker, Dizzy Gillespie, Thelonius Monk, and others. Charlie Chisholm's Boss-Tet released *Cooking at the Cadillac Club* in 1968. The Boss-Tet was formed in 1965 by Chisholm and Frank Gatlin. Featured on the album are Chisholm, trumpet and flugelhorn; Gatlin, alto and tenor saxophone; Kenny Lowe, piano; Floyd Brace, bass; and Tommy Pinkett, drums. (Courtesy of Charles L. Blockson Afro-American Collection, Temple University Libraries.)

Donald Wilson (1936–2012) pianist, composer, arranger, bandleader, and instructor, was a member of the Tommy Monroe Big Band, which included Johnny Coles, John Coltrane, Lee Morgan, Bobby Timmons, Albert "Tootie" Heath, Reggie Workman, Archie Shepp, and others. He also backed musicians such as Harold Vick, Sonny Stitt, Art Farmer, and others. Wilson started a big band in 1975 and later served as musical director and conductor of the Philadelphia Clef Club big band. He taught music instruction at Temple University and Mount Airy Cultural Center. From left to right are (first row) jazz radio personality Bob Perkins, tenor saxophonist Bootsie Barnes, club owner Dr. La Rose, drummer Leon Jordan Sr., jazz vocalist Miss Justine, pianist Don Wilson, and alto saxophonist Tony Williams; (second row) jazz vocalist Ella Ghant, bassist Mike Boone, and tenor saxophonist Tim Warfield at La Rose Jazz Club around the 2000s. (Photograph by Millicent G. Muse, courtesy of Charles L. Blockson Afro-American Collection, Temple University Libraries.)

Bassist Lonnie Edward "Ed" Crockett (1942–2010) was active for over 30 years on Philadelphia's local scene, working with Odean Pope and Byard Lancaster. An integral part of the band The Visitors with saxophonists Earl and Carl Grubbs and pianist Sid Simmons, Crockett also recorded the influential album *The Philadelphia Spirit in New York*. Pictured here is one of his local performances around the 1980s. (Courtesy of Charles L. Blockson Afro-American Collection, Temple University Libraries.)

Donald Washington Sr. (1930–2009), tenor saxophonist, bandleader, and teacher, was referred to in Philadelphia as the "Father of the Saxophone." He founded the Marlboro Men and traveled to Jamaica, Haiti, and the Virgin Islands. He performed with Nat King Cole, Sammy Davis Jr., Horace Silver, Donald Byrd, and others. He was music director of the *Al Copeland Review*. Charles Fambrough, Grover Washington Jr., and George Howard were among his students. Pictured here is Donald Washington performing around the 1990s. (Courtesy of photographer Paul Somerville.)

Alfred McCoy Tyner (1938–2020), pianist, composer, and bandleader, was born in Philadelphia and studied at the Granoff School of Music. The groundbreaking pianist was a member of the famous John Coltrane Quartet. After leaving Coltrane's band, he quickly established himself as a leader with his debut album for Blue Note, *The Real McCoy*, with drummer Elvin Jones, saxophonist Joe Henderson, and bassist Ron Carter. Pictured here is McCoy Tyner being honored at the Philadelphia Clef Club while "Cousin Mary" Alexander (John Coltrane's cousin) congratulates him in the 2000s. The bassist pictured in the background is Christian McBride. (Photograph by Bruce Turner, courtesy of Charles L. Blockson Afro-American Collection, Temple University Libraries.)

Donald "Don" Gardner (1931–2018), singer, drummer, and bandleader, led a group called the Three Bachelors, later renamed the Sonotones. His early recordings were a training ground for Jimmy Smith and Grover Washington Jr. He performed, travelled and recorded R&B hits with singer/keyboardist Dee Ford and vocalist Justine "Baby" Washington. He also served as road manager for Curtis Mayfield. In the early 1990s, he was elected board president of the Philadelphia Clef Club of Jazz & Performing Arts. Pictured from left to right, Don Gardner sings accompanied by organist Shirley Scott and tenor saxophonist Bootsie Barnes at Temple University in the 1990s. (Photograph by Bruce Turner, courtesy of Charles L. Blockson Afro-American Collection, Temple University Libraries.)

Trudy Pitts (1933–2010), pianist, organist, vocalist, composer, and educator, studied at Juilliard and crossed over into jazz, performing on the B-3 organ with her future husband, Bill "Mr. C" Carney, along with John Coltrane and Tootie Heath. She recorded *Introducing the Fabulous Trudy Pitts* with sidemen Mr. C and Pat Martino. Pitts recorded on Martino's 1967 debut album *El Hombre* for Prestige. Trudy Pitts mentored students at the University of the Arts as an adjunct associate professor. Drummer Mr. C and his wife, pianist Trudy Pitts, are pictured at their weekly Sunday brunch gig at the Meiji-E in the 1990s. (Photograph by Bruce Turner, courtesy of Charles L. Blockson Afro-American Collection, Temple University Libraries.)

Thelma Anderson (1928–2017), a lifelong friend of saxophonist and composer Benny Golson, founded the Council of Jazz Advocates in 1990 to sponsor and promote jazz events and public school musicians and to advocate for jazz programs on television and radio. She was a major supporter of the Tony Williams Jazz Festival and was on the board of the Mount Airy Cultural Society. From left to right, bandleader and baritone saxophonist Joe Sudler, alto saxophonist Tony Williams, and jazz enthusiast and promoter Thelma Anderson attend a Jazz People's Collective event at Rhythm's Club around the 1990s. (Patented Photos, courtesy of Diane D. Turner.)

Pictured from left to right are trumpeter Messiah Harley, Mill Creek Cultural Center producer Ronald Dewey Wynne, Trane Stop founder Arnold Boyd, and bagpipe player Rufus Harley attending a Jazz People's Collective event at Rhythm's Club around the 1990s. (Patented Photos, courtesy of Diane D. Turner.)

Pictured from left to right, Shirley Scott, piano; Tim Warfield, tenor saxophone; Arthur Harper, bass; and Mickey Roker, drums, perform at Mill Creek Cultural Center around the 1990s. (Photograph by Bruce Turner, courtesy of Charles L. Blockson Afro-American Collection, Temple University Libraries.)

Pictured from left to right are pianist Uri Caine, bassist Tyrone Brown, tenor saxophonist Bootsie Barnes, jazz producer Bill Cosby, alto saxophonist Tony Williams, and drummer Mickey Roker on tour with Cosby in 1986. (Courtesy of Charles L. Blockson Afro-American Collection, Temple University Libraries.)

Theodore "Ted" Curson (1935–2012) trumpeter, flugelhornist, and bandleader, graduated from Mastbaum Vocational Technical High School. He played with Charlie Mingus, Cecil Taylor, and Eric Dolphy and recorded 18 albums as a leader on Atlantic, Columbia, and Prestige Records. Curson is pictured on trumpet with house band leader Bootsie Barnes at T'N'T Monroe's around the 1980s. (Courtesy of Charles L. Blockson Afro-American Collection, Temple University Libraries.)

Organist Emmett "Lumpy" King was a mainstay at Natalie's and can be heard on the album *Friday, Saturday, Monday* by Nate Wiley and the Crowd Pleasers. He is pictured in the 1990s. (Photograph by Pedro J. Matos, courtesy of Charles L. Blockson Afro-American Collection, Temple University Libraries.)

Clarinetist Buddy DeFranco (1923–2014) was born in Camden, New Jersey, and raised in South Philadelphia. DeFranco recorded over 50 albums as a leader and many more as a sideman for other leading jazz artists, including Lionel Hampton, Count Basie, Billie Holiday, and Ella Fitzgerald. While swing-era clarinetists faded away, DeFranco was one of the few who was comfortable playing bebop. (Courtesy of the William Gottlieb Collection, Library of Congress.)

Wilber Ware, double bassist (1923–1979), was born in Chicago and later moved to Philadelphia. After his military service during World War II, he played with Roy Eldridge, Sonny Stitt, Stuff Smith and others in Chicago. He recorded with Big Bill Broonzy, Johnny Perry, Johnny Griffin, and Junior Nance. In New York, Ware performed or recorded, mainly on the Riverside and Blue Note labels, with Art Blakey, Thelonious Monk, John Coltrane, Sonny Rollins, Lee Morgan, Kenny Drew, Zoot Sims, Buddy DeFranco, Hank Mobley, Kenny Dorham, Tina Brooks, Clifford Jordan, Grant Green, Blue Mitchell, Elvin Jones, Archie Shepp, and others. (Photograph by Martin Bough, courtesy of Gloria Ware.)

Bill Barron (1927–1989), tenor and soprano saxophonist, educator, and older brother of pianist Kenny Barron, recorded with Cecil Taylor, Philly Joe Jones, and as leader on Savoy Records. He is pictured in 1986. (Courtesy of Northeastern University Library.)

Seven

All in the Jazz Family

The Philadelphia region has boasted a few important jazz families, some multigenerational and some that consist of siblings growing up together with music surrounding them. One of the most prominent jazz families were the Heath brothers, who grew up at 1927 Federal Street in South Philadelphia. Bassist Percy Heath, the eldest, saxophonist Jimmy Heath, the middle child, and drummer Albert "Tootie" Heath grew up in a home full of music, and many jazz musicians like John Coltrane and Dizzy Gillespie played the sessions held there. Saxophonist Benny Golson remembers, "Enough cannot be said about Mr. and Mrs. Heath . . . who continuously put up with all of us. . . . [We'd] remove all of the furniture in the living and dining room, then begin our rehearsal. No matter what we did, how much noise (music) we made or how late we did it, they were always our champions. It was their support that, in part, enabled us to grow. And grow we did."

Philadelphia jazz pianist and composer Ray Bryant was born into a musical home in 1931. His brothers, bassist Tommy and singer/drummer Len, were all professional jazz musicians, and his multi-instrumentalist sister Vera taught jazz pianist Kenny Barron (younger brother of saxophonist Bill Barron and future National Endowment for the Arts Jazz Master). Vera Bryant married and became Vera Eubanks, later giving birth at 6340 Milton Street in the Mount Airy neighborhood of Philadelphia to three jazz artists of note: guitarist Kevin Eubanks, trombonist Robin Eubanks, and trumpeter Duane Eubanks.

There were a few other important jazz families in the greater metro area, like the Dockery family of Camden, New Jersey, which gave the city pianist Sam Dockery and bassist Wayne Dockery, and the Brecker brothers, trumpeter Randy and saxophonist Michael from Cheltenham. But the Heath brothers and the extended Bryant/Eubanks family established a historical and generational jazz legacy that influenced so many of the musicians who played and grew up with them.

Pictured from left to right are saxophonist Gary Bartz, jazz vocalist and drummer Don Gardner, and pianist Ray Bryant at the Philadelphia Clef Club around 1990. (Photograph by Bruce Turner, courtesy of Charles L. Blockson Afro-American Collection, Temple University Libraries.)

Pianist Vera Eubanks, mother of Eubanks brothers (Kevin, Robin, and Duane) and sister of pianist Ray Bryant, is seen here teaching the future jazz pianist Kenny Barron (about eight years old). (Courtesy of the Eubanks family collection.)

Pictured here are the Heath brothers, bassist Percy Heath, saxophonist Jimmy Heath, and drummer Albert "Tootie" Heath, performing at the University of Pennsylvania in the 1990s. (Photograph by Bruce Turner, courtesy of Charles L. Blockson Afro-American Collection, Temple University Libraries.)

Pictured here, tenor saxophonist Michael Brecker and trumpeter Randy Brecker, known as the Brecker Brothers, perform at Penn's Landing in the 1990s. (Photograph by Bruce Turner, courtesy of Charles L. Blockson Afro-American Collection, Temple University Libraries.)

Bassist Wayne Dockery (1941–2018) was born in Camden, the younger brother of Sam Dockery and drummer Lemuel Dockery, who worked and recorded with George Benson, Sonny Fortune, Eddie Henderson, Hal Galper, Archie Shepp, Michael Brecker, and others. He is pictured at Jazz Festival St. Ingbert in 1990. (Courtesy of photographer Walter Gehring.)

Pianist Samuel "Sam" Dockery (1929–2015) became a regular at Ellis Tollins's Music City store, where local musicians played with visiting jazz greats. He caught the attention of Buddy Rich and was invited to tour with his orchestra from 1955 to 1956. He returned to Music City, where members of Art Blakey's Jazz Messengers heard him. He was hired and toured with the band from 1956 to 1957. He recorded with Blakey, composing "Sam's Tune" on 1957's *Ritual* for Blue Note. He became a permanent pianist at the Show Boat, playing with Sonny Stitt, Gene Ammons, Kenny Dorham, Jimmy Heath, Esther Phillips, Lorez Alexandria, and others. He also performed with Betty Carter at Birdland and toured with the Roy Haynes Band. He taught at the University of the Arts and trained church choirs. Dockery featured in the 2011 Jazzy in July Concert Series, staged by executive director Sandra Turner-Barnes for the Camden County Cultural & Heritage Commission. (Photograph by Pedro J. Matos, courtesy of Charles L. Blockson Afro-American Collection, Temple University Libraries.)

Eight

Hard Bop City

Charlie Parker and Dizzy Gillespie were the major architects of bebop, and because Dizzy spent his formative years in Philly, many local legends were influenced by him. After the death of Charlie Parker, bebop changed direction with the development of hard bop. The music began incorporating rhythm and blues, gospel, and the blues, and hard bop became a dominant genre of jazz from about 1955 to 1965, especially in Philadelphia. Some credit drummer Art Blakey and pianist Horace Silver with the initial fusion of funky African American rhythms with the instrumental complexities of bebop. Blakey's iconic album *Hard Bop* included Philly musicians pianist Sam Dockery and bassist Spanky DeBrest in 1956, but Blakey did not stop there, hiring many musicians from Philly, which fast became hard bop's hometown. In 1958, Blakey hired trumpeter Lee Morgan, pianist Bobby Timmons, saxophonist Benny Golson, and bassist Jymie Merritt for his band—all Philadelphians.

Other noted jazz musicians from the city who performed hard bop included trumpeter Clifford Brown, saxophonist Bootsie Barnes, pianist Kenny Barron, saxophonist John Coltrane, trumpeter Ted Curson, the Heath brothers, drummer Philly Joe Jones, guitarist Pat Martino, saxophonist Hank Mobley, pianist Richie Powell, organists Trudy Pitts, Jimmy Smith, and Shirley Scott, pianist McCoy Tyner, and bassists Buster Williams and Reggie Workman.

Places that featured this brand of bop included the Blue Note on Ridge Avenue, the Red Hill Inn in Pennsauken, New Jersey, Pep's Musical Bar, the Show Boat, Jewel's at 679 North Broad Street, the Philadelphia Clef Club, Aqua Lounge, Nat Seagal's Downbeat Club, and Music City. But many of the clubs in the city nurturing this new soul jazz were small neighborhood venues with a loyal clientele that gave the musicians the room to stretch and create over the years up to and including today, clubs such as Natalie's, T'N'T Monroe's, Second Story, Slim Cooper's, La Rose Jazz and Supper Club, L.G.'s Blue Note, Bob and Barbara's, Ortlieb's Jazzhaus, and the Saloon in Camden, New Jersey.

Charles Fambrough (1950–2011), bassist, composer, and record producer, was a member of Art Blakey's Jazz Messengers. He formed his own quintet. He was a member of the house band led by Bootsie Barnes at Tommy Monroe's club T'N'T Monroe's, located at 1433 Arch Street. He also played with Freddie Hubbard, Airto Moreira and Shirley Scott. Pictured are bassist Charles Fambrough (left) and bassist Stanley Clarke (right). (Photograph by Bruce Turner, courtesy of Charles L. Blockson Afro-American Collection, Temple University Libraries.)

This publicity photograph for Art Blakey and his Jazz Messengers includes all Philadelphia players. From left to right are Art Blakey, Benny Golson, Bobby Timmons, Lee Morgan, and Jymie Merritt. This photograph was taken in Rochester, New York, at the Ridge Crest Inn in October 1958 just before their first tour. (Courtesy of photographer Paul Hoeffler, CTS Images.)

Drummer William Rudolph "Philly Joe" Jones (1923–1985) played with many bands in Philly. Prior to moving to New York in 1947, he became one of the first eight Blacks to operate trolley cars after the 1944 Philadelphia Transportation Company strike. In New York, Jones worked with Dizzy Gillespie, Dexter Gordon, Fats Navarro, and Charlie Parker. Later, he played with Miles Davis, Lee Konitz, Zoot Sims, and Tadd Dameron. In the late 1960s, he taught in London and Paris. In the 1970s, he returned to Philadelphia and formed Le Grand Prix, a jazz-rock group. Pictured here is Philly Joe Jones performing on WBGO's *Live from the Big Apple* series at the Jazz Forum in New York City with Larry Ridley on the edge by the cymbal, c.1990s. (Photograph by Bill May, courtesy of Charles L. Blockson Afro-American Collection, Temple University Libraries.)

Guitarist Patrick C. Azzara, also known as Pat Martino (1944–2021), came from a musical background. His father sang and briefly studied guitar with Eddie Lang. Martino studied music with Dennis Sandole and was also influenced by Wes Montgomery. His first jazz tour was with Charles Earland, and he later worked with Slide Hampton, Lloyd Price, Red Holloway, Jack McDuff, Don Patterson, Trudy Pitts, Jimmy Smith, Joey DeFrancesco, Richard "Groove" Holmes, and others. Here Martino performs at the Central Pennsylvania Festival of Jazz around the 1990s. (Photograph by Bruce Turner, courtesy of Charles L. Blockson Afro-American Collection, Temple University Libraries.)

Pictured behind trumpeter Lee Morgan, bassist James A. "Spanky" DeBrest Jr. (1937–1973) was one of Philly's finest. He majored in music at Benjamin Franklin High School and matriculated at the University of Pennsylvania. He recorded with Art Blakey, J.J. Johnson, Donald Byrd, Betty Carter, Anita O'Day, Thelonious Monk, Evelyn Simms, Philly Joe Jones, Jackie McClean, John Coltrane, Lee Morgan, Harold Corbin, and others. Lee Morgan was still a teenager when DeBrest was in the rhythm section of the virtuoso trumpeter's earliest Philly band. DeBrest is pictured at the Cotton Club in Atlantic City in 1955 with McCoy Tyner (unseen) and Lee Morgan. (Courtesy of the McCoy Tyner Archives.)

Bassist James Emory "Jimmy" Garrison (1934–1976) worked locally with Cal Massey, Tommy Monroe, John Coltrane, and McCoy Tyner. In New York, Garrison performed with Curtis Fuller, Bill Evans, Philly Joe Jones, Kenny Dorham, Ornette Coleman, Tony Scott, and Lennie Tristano. He played with the famous Coltrane Quartet and toured with Elvin Jones and Archie Shepp. (Photograph by Ornette Dolphy.)

Tenor saxophonist Hank Mobley (1930–1986) was one of the most important hard bop players and composers in the 1950s and 1960s. He took part in one of the earliest hard bop sessions, alongside Art Blakey, Horace Silver, Doug Watkins, and trumpeter Kenny Dorham. From 1956 to 1970, Mobley recorded as a leader for Blue Note Records. Unfortunately, many of his albums were not released by the record company until after his death, which hurt his legacy. He is pictured here with trumpeter Art Farmer. (Courtesy of photographer William "PoPsie" Randolph, December 28, 1956, in NYC.)

Wallace Roney (1950–2020), trumpeter, composer, and bandleader, studied at the Settlement School of Music, the Duke Ellington School of the Arts, Howard University, and Berklee College of Music. At 15, he debuted on Haki Madhubuti and Nation: Afrikan Liberation Arts Ensemble's recording *Rise Vision Comin* in 1971. His mentors included Clark Terry, Dizzy Gillespie, and Miles Davis, who influenced his life and music career. At 16, he played with the Cedar Walton Quartet. Roney played and recorded with Art Blakey's Jazz Messengers, Miles Davis, Elvin Jones, Wayne Shorter, Philly Joe Jones, Herbie Hancock, Sonny Rollins, Tony Williams, David Murray, McCoy Tyner, and many others. He recorded nearly 20 albums as a leader. Here Roney performs at Penn's Landing with Miles Davis' horn in the 1990s. (Photograph by Bruce Turner, courtesy of Charles L. Blockson Afro-American Collection, Temple University Libraries.)

Organist Jack McDuff (1926–2001) settled in Philadelphia after being discharged from the US Army. He performed with John Coltrane and other local musicians. In 2001, he recorded the album *Brotherly Love*, which included Pat Martino and Joey DeFrancesco. Pictured from left to right are trombonist Clifford Adams, tenor saxophonist Larry McKenna, and Jack McDuff around the 1990s. (Photograph by Bruce Turner, courtesy of Charles L. Blockson Afro-American Collection, Temple University Libraries.)

Nine

Voices of Jazz

Philadelphia has always had a plethora of singers who bravely took the stage in every established musical genre and venue. Jazz was no different. From early on, the city exploded with stars who found that the segregated black and white theaters and clubs were eager to showcase their talents. Cecil "Kid Haffey" Collier, who had worked with the giants of big band jazz back in the day, would go on to record with Zoot Sims and Al Cohn in 1961 on an album produced by jazz writer Fred Miles. Haffey later would bartend at Pep's Musical Showbar and sing with many small ensemble bands there. George "Bon Bon" Tunnell sang with Philadelphian Jan Savitt's Top Hatters band in the 1930s and 1940s. The beautiful Dottie Smith was a presence in the city in the 1950s and 1960s before she was hustled off to the West Coast for a screen test to possibly play Billie Holiday in film. Ruth Price was discovered at Music City and quickly headed to New York City, eventually founding the iconic venue Jazz Bakery in Los Angeles. Evelyn Simms, a mainstay at the Underground club in Center City in the 1960s, started her career by sitting in with Benny Field's band at Mercantile Hall when she was a young teen. Her girlfriend told Benny that Evelyn sang much better than his regular singer! Simms laughingly told *Philadelphia Daily News* writer Jack Lloyd that, at the time, she didn't know the men playing behind her were Bill Doggett, Benny Golson, Johnny Coles, and John Coltrane. Donna Jean, a regular player at the Borgia Café with pianist Bob Cohen and bassist Tyrone Brown, eventually taught voice at Temple University. Singer Nina Bundy regularly appeared with Shirley Scott and her trio at Ortlieb's Jazzhaus; vocalists Clyde Terrell and Juanita Holiday were frequently seen at Zanzibar Blue at Eleventh and Pine Streets with the Eddie Green Trio, with blues singer Zan Gardner holding forth on Sunday brunches there. Sarah Dean and the Metropole Jazz Band seemed to be everywhere in town; she billed herself as the "last of the red-hot mamas." One cannot forget Kitty Kallen, who scored hits with the big bands of Artie Shaw, Tommy Dorsey, and Harry James. She quit Dorsey's band because she believed him to be anti-Semitic but then went on to make top-ten hits as a single artist after the big bands faded. It is difficult in this small space to highlight every jazz singer who found their first audiences in Philly, but many unique talents made this city sound so, so fine.

Cecil "Kid Haffey" Collier (?–1975), who received his nickname playing halfback with the old Philadelphia Steamrollers football team, was often referred to as "Philadelphia's Jimmy Rushing." He was frequently seen at the Blue Note on Ridge Avenue working as a bouncer and bartender. He recorded an important album called *Either Way* in 1961 for the Fred Miles Presents label with Zoot Simms and Al Cohn. (Courtesy of Fred Miles Presents.)

Doreatha "Dottie" Smith (1925–2012), singer and conga/snare player, started her career as a child performing on Philadelphia's original *Colored Kiddies Hour*. She sang with the Harlemaires at the Baby Grant Night Club in New York. Smith recorded and toured with the Louis Jordan Tympany Five, headlining at the Earle Theatre. Jordan heard her perform at Spider Kelly's and offered her a job on the spot. She also performed, toured, or was associated with Beryl Booker, Dinah Washington, Errol Garner, Nat King Cole, Sammy David Jr., and Dinah Shore. Smith appeared on television shows hosted by Ed Sullivan, Steve Allen, Patti Page, and Perry Como. (Courtesy of Charles L. Blockson Afro-American Collection, Temple University Libraries.)

Katherine "Kitty" De Chavis (1919–2021), jazz singer and dancer, started her singing career at St. Peter Clavier's Church in South Philly. She also sang on the *Colored Kiddie Hour* at Lincoln Theatre. She performed with Nat King Cole and George Shearing and toured with Lena Horne, Earl Bostic, and others. She made the first vocal recording of "Hucklebuck." This promotional photograph is from the 1940s. (Courtesy of Charles L. Blockson Afro-American Collection, Temple University Libraries.)

Evelyn Simms (?–2002), a singer known as "Mama Diva," was born in Odom, Georgia, and came to Philadelphia as a child. Simms first sang at the Mercantile Hall with the Benny Fields band when she was prodded by her girlfriends to sit in. She was a hit and soon made her professional debut at the age of 16 with pianist Ray Bryant. She went on to work with Dizzy Gillespie's big band, Erskine Hawkins, Bobby Durham, Jimmy Golden, Gerald Price, Tommy Flanagan, and Barry Harris. She met her closest friend, Shirley Scott, when they were both with Coatesville Harris. Simms received best artist and best recording awards from the Philadelphia Music Alliance for her only album, *On My Own* for Encounter Records (later Dreambox Media), in 1988. (Courtesy of her granddaughter Danielle Shaw.)

Ruth Mobley (1925–2017), vocalist and cocktail drummer, toured with top entertainers. She was the longtime treasurer of the Philadelphia Clef Club. (Courtesy of Diane D. Turner.)

Katie "Kitty" Kallen (1921–2016), a singer born and raised in Philadelphia by Russian Jewish immigrants, began singing as a child on *The Children's Hour*, a radio show sponsored by the Horn & Hardart company, which led to her having a program on WCAU. She started singing in big bands at the age of 15, first with the Jan Savitt band and then with Artie Shaw, Tommy Dorsey, Harry James, and Jack Teagarden. She is widely known for her 1954 solo recording "Little Things Mean a Lot," a song that stayed at the US Billboard number-one spot for nine consecutive weeks and took top honor as 1954's number-one song of the year. (Courtesy of Suzanne Cloud.)

Nina Bundy (1937–2012) started singing at an early age with her mother. Recognized as a fully throated jazz singer, Bundy played all the clubs and festivals in the northeastern states and Japan. Frequently, she performed in the all-star diva format with Miss Justine and Rhetta Morgan. Her last album, called *Simply Natural*, was released in 2005. Bundy is pictured with trumpeter Winston Byrd. (Photograph by Ben Johnson, courtesy of Charles L. Blockson Afro-American Collection, Temple University Libraries.)

Singer and actress Juanita Holiday (1942–2016) started singing at six. Her vocal styles included jazz, blues, and gospel. Holiday performed at Zanzibar Blue for six years and sang at the Cape May Jazz Festival, the Mellon Jazz Festival, the Philadelphia Art Museum, the Mann Music Center, and other venues in Philadelphia. She is pictured in a c. 1990s promotional photograph. (Courtesy of Diane D. Turner.)

Billy Paul (1934–2016), heavily influenced by female jazz vocalists such as Billie Holiday and Nina Simone, studied at the West Philadelphia Music School and the Granoff School of Music. After a stint in the service, Paul formed a jazz trio with hard bop pianist Sam Dockery and bassist Buster Williams. In 1959, he joined the New Dawn record label and released the single "Ebony Woman" backed with "You Go to Hell," both written by Morris Bailey Jr. In 1960, Paul recorded "I'm Always a Brother," written by Leon Mitchell and Charles Gaston. His career took off when he started recording for Kenny Gamble and Leon Huff of Philadelphia International Records. Billy Paul had a huge Grammy-winning hit with "Me and Mrs. Jones," backed by pianist Eddie Green and bassist Tyrone Brown. Paul performs at Penn's Landing in the 1990s. (Photograph by Bruce Turner, courtesy of Charles L. Blockson Afro-American Collection, Temple University Libraries.)

Nathan Ingram III (1950–2012), vocal coach, producer, and singer, not only performed in clubs in the Philadelphia region such as Crawford's, Rhythm's, and La Rose Jazz Club but also produced concerts and participated in jazz workshops and seminars. Ingram's second home was in Japan, where he taught African American music courses to broaden the appreciation of jazz. Ingram performs at Ortlieb's Jazzhaus with pianist Lucas Brown around the 1990s. (Photograph by Pedro J. Matos, courtesy of Diane D. Turner.)

In 1957, guitarist and singer Jimi Odell worked with the Red Fox show at the Cotton Club, and he went on to play with almost every musician from the Philadelphia–New Jersey area over the years. He taught himself the guitar from books at the age of 19 and promptly started lining up gigs. But it wasn't his guitar playing that brought the people in, it was his singing, especially his scatting. Jimi can be heard scatting with Lionel Hampton, Tony Williams, and Jim Martinez's group on the album *Jazz Praise II*. Odell's album *Jamming at 23rd Street* was heralded by *Tempo* magazine as one in which "the guitar speaks volumes, and his vocals range from heartbreaking tenderness to danceable scat." (Photograph by Bruce Turner, courtesy of Charles L. Blockson Afro-American Collection, Temple University Libraries.)

Ten

FREE JAZZ PHILLY

As some of the popularity of the hard bop scene was giving way to John Coltrane's explorations in free jazz in the 1960s, Philadelphia was again home to many artists playing this new and innovative music. Musicians like bassist Henry Grimes and drummer Rashied Ali were already playing in some legendary free jazz ensembles, yet while some Philly jazz musicians were dedicating themselves to this new, revolutionary music, the city's local scene did not allow much room for free jazz to thrive. However, the Germantown neighborhood exploded with the new music in the 1970s with Sun Ra and his Arkestra moving into their house at 5626 Morton Street in 1968. Major players like vibraphonist Khan Jamal and saxophonist Byard Lancaster lived in the neighborhood and made Germantown their base of operations, even though both musicians were very well known and appreciated all over the world. The *Philadelphia Daily News* jazz writer Nels Nelson wrote of Lancaster, "If all the music bursting to get out of him were to escape in one instant, NASA would pick up Byardic shards in the rings of Saturn." Lancaster joined forces with Khan Jamal in the band Sounds of Liberation in 1970, and their music was considered a social movement that placed the ensemble "at the forefront of avant-garde Black expression," according to Ars Nova Workshop when the group appeared at their October Revolution Festival in 2019. The group issued one self-released album, *New Horizons*, in 1972, which did not get too much notice until it was rereleased in 2019 by Dogtown Records just before a reunion concert opening for Marshall Allen and the Sun Ra Arkestra. The main place to hear free jazz for many years was at Geno's Empty Foxhole, which opened on Christmas Day in 1970. Situated in the lower level of the parish hall of St. Mary's Church on the campus of the University of Pennsylvania, the small space played host to Sun Ra, Rufus Harley, Charles Mingus, Rahsaan Roland Kirk, Cecil Taylor, the Art Ensemble of Chicago, and Archie Shepp. Other venues that catered to the free jazz crowd were the Mill Creek Community Center on Lancaster Avenue, the Painted Bride Art Center, and Grendel's Lair on South Street.

John William Coltrane (1926–1967), jazz saxophonist and composer also known as "Trane," started his career playing bebop and hard bop but quickly revolutionized jazz with his breakout album *Giant Steps*. He helped pioneer the use of modes in jazz and was later at the forefront of free jazz. He organized at least 50 recording sessions as a leader during his career and appeared as a sideman on many other albums, notably with trumpeter Miles Davis and pianist Thelonious Monk. The famous John Coltrane Quartet is pictured here in 1963, just before a concert in Stockholm, Sweden. From left to right are drummer Alvin Jones, pianist McCoy Tyner, tenor and soprano saxophonist John Coltrane, and bassist Jimmy Garrison. (Courtesy of *Aftonbladet*.)

Pianist and composer Hasaan Ibn Ali was seen by many as the "Thelonious Monk of Philadelphia" because of his imaginative and eclectic approach to music. According to pianist Matthew Shipp, "Hasaan is in some ways a forerunner of Coltrane—with his own sheets of sound, large and long groupings of notes that he scrambles across the keyboard, which can resolve into any harmonic sequence. So there are fragments of bebop lines as we know them, interspersed with Hasaan's own version of sheets of sound that all accumulate until we reach a density of sound that is orchestral in scope." Ibn Ali mentored saxophonist Odean Pope, and Pope helped orchestrate the remastering and publication of this Philadelphia legend's last recording, which was thought to be destroyed in the famous Atlantic Records/MGM fire in 1972. It is now an album called *Metaphysics: The Lost Atlantic Album*. Ibn Ali is pictured at the Purple Onion in Greenwich Village in 1965. (Courtesy of photographer Alan Sukoenig.)

Le Sony'r Ra was born Herman Poole Blount (1914–1993). Sun Ra's sojourn in Philadelphia began in 1968, when the New York building his Arkestra was renting was put up for sale. Sun Ra and the Arkestra relocated to Morton Street in the Germantown section of Philadelphia. The friendliness of the band, their drug-free living, and their rapport with youngsters made them good neighbors. When lightning struck a tree on their street, Sun Ra took it as a good omen. Sun Ra became a fixture in Philadelphia, appearing semiregularly on WXPN radio, giving lectures to community groups, or visiting the city's libraries. In the mid-1970s, the Arkestra sometimes played free Saturday afternoon concerts in parks near their home. Pictured here is Sun Ra at Vernon Park, Philadelphia, in 1974. (Courtesy of photographer H. Alonzo Jennings.)

Marshall Allen, clarinetist, alto saxophonist and bandleader, leads the Sun Ra Arkestra. They called their rowhome in Philadelphia "The Pharaoh's Den." Allen helped Sun Ra run the band, rehearsing Monday through Sunday until Ra's death in 1993, and Allen has led the Arkestra ever since, constantly exploring and reexploring the immense musical output of the late pioneer of Afrofuturism. (Photograph by Bruce Turner, courtesy of Charles L. Blockson Afro-American Collection, Temple University Libraries.)

Byard Lancaster (1942–2012), alto saxophonist, flutist, bass clarinetist, and educator, started playing piano at four years old before moving to saxophone. Influenced by John Coltrane and others, he first made his mark in the New York avant-garde jazz scene. He performed on drummer Sunny Murray and trumpeter Bill Dixon's landmark recordings. He also played with the Sun Ra Arkestra, McCoy Tyner, and Odean Pope's Saxophone Choir. He mentored bassist Stanley Clarke, saxophonist Jaleel Shaw, and keyboardist Kamal Gray of the Roots. During the 1980s and 1990s, he taught in Jamaica and Lagos, Nigeria. Lancaster performs at Lex Humphries's memorial. (Courtesy Diane D. Turner.)

Middy Middleton, saxophonist and composer, recorded and played with Odean Pope's Saxophone Choir, Sunny Murray, and the John Minis Big Bone Band. Middleton formed his own group in the 1970s called the Renaissance Band with guitarist Monnette Sudler and trumpeter Warren Carter. From left to right are tenor/soprano saxophonist Middy Middleton, drummer Billy James, and bartender Otto Brown at Ortlieb's Jazzhaus. (Photograph by Bruce Turner, courtesy of Charles L. Blockson Afro-American Collection, Temple University Libraries.)

Khan Jamal (1946–2022), vibraphonist, marimba player, percussionist, composer, and bandleader, attended the Granoff School of Music with Bill Lewis and Combs College of Music with William Walton. He became a key musician of avant-garde jazz during the 1970s and 1980s in Philadelphia. He performed with John Lewis, Archie Shepp, David Murray, Jimmy Smith, Philly Joe Jones, Reggie Workman, Odean Pope, Granchan Moncur, Sunny Murray, Monnette Sudler, Grover Washington Jr., and many others. He has recorded and performed with one of his earliest mentors, Byard Lancaster, and with Jamaldeen Tecuma, Billy Hart, Omar Hill, Oliver Collins, Clifton Burton, and others. Here Jamal performs at the Mirage Supper Club in Newark, New Jersey, in 1985. (Photograph by Bill May, courtesy of Charles L. Blockson Afro-American Collection, Temple University Libraries.)

Daniel P. "Dan" Jones (1940–) bassoonist, tenor saxophonist, bandleader, freelance photographer, and educator, received his early musical education at Mastbaum High School. He performed with Rashid Ali, Curtis Fuller, Sun Ra, Cal Massey, Sam Reed, Leon Mitchell, Alice Coltrane, Wilbur Ware, Gary Bartz, Reggie Workman, Jimmy Heath, and others. Jones also founded the House of Dan, where he held performances, workshops, seminars, and open discussions on contemporary music by Black composers in the Philadelphia region. He operated the Dan Jones Studio at 3728 Germantown Avenue, offering classes and instruction in theory, harmony, composition, and the legalities of the music business. Jones also taught a music appreciation class at the Parkway School. (Courtesy of Diane D. Turner.)

Cornelius "Sonny" Fortune (1939–2018), soprano, alto, tenor, and baritone saxophonist, studied at the Granoff School of Music. John Coltrane was his friend and mentor in Philly. He performed and recorded with Coltrane, Mongo Santamaria, Leon Thomas, Nat Adderley, Buddy Rich, Buster Williams, Jimmy Cobb, Mike Stern, John Hicks, Kirk Lightsey, Santi Debriano, Jeff "Tain" Watts, Eddie Henderson, Joe Lovano, Charles Sullivan, Stanley Cowell, and others. He performs at the Afro-American Historical and Culture Museum in Philadelphia in 1994. (Photograph by Bruce Turner, courtesy of Charles L. Blockson Afro-American Collection, Temple University Libraries.)

Drummer Rashied Ali (1933–2009) was a student of Philly Joe Jones. He started his career in the US Army then toured with Sonny Rollins. He played with Lee Morgan, Don Patterson, and Jimmy Smith in Philly. In the 1960s, he went to New York and performed with Don Cherry, Paul Bley, Pharoah Sanders, Albert Ayler, Bill Dixon, John Coltrane, and others. He recorded or performed with Archie Shepp, Jackie McLean, Gary Bartz, Dewey Redman, Alice Coltrane, and numerous other musicians. During the 1970s, Ali opened Ali's Alley, a loft–jazz club, and Survival Records, highlighting avant-garde jazz. (Photograph by Bruce Turner, courtesy of Charles L. Blockson Afro-American Collection, Temple University Libraries.)

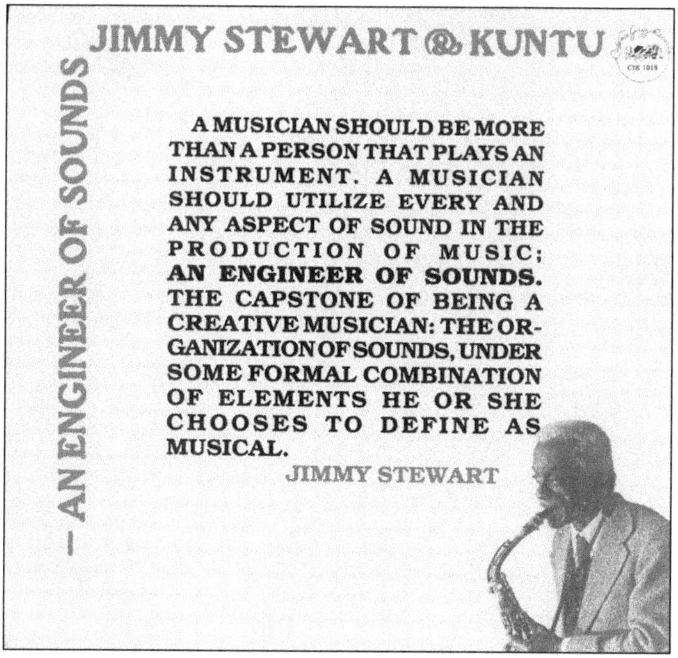

James "Jimmy" Stewart, clarinetist, baritone and alto saxophonist, and producer, played in the house band of the Uptown Theatre under the leadership of Doc Bagby and as assistant leader in the Charlie Chisholm Big Band. In 1968, Kuntu was formed and performed at a concert of Black music and poetry at the Lee Cultural Center. Jimmy Stewart and Kuntu released *An Engineer of Sounds* in 1984. Stewart was a member of the free jazz movement. (Courtesy of Charles L. Blockson Afro-American Collection, Temple University Libraries.)

Sounds of Liberation was a jazz collective established in 1970 in the Germantown section of Philadelphia in the midst of the Black Arts Movement. They performed at community events, in prisons, and for schoolchildren. The collective released the album New Horizons in 1972 and recorded a session at Columbia University in 1973. From left to right are reed player Byard Lancaster, bassist Billy Mills, guitarist Monnette Sudler, drummer Dwight James, vibist Khan Jamal, and percussionist Rashid Salim IV. (Courtesy of Dogtown Records.)

BIBLIOGRAPHY

Berger, Edward. *Softly, with Feeling: Joe Wilder and the Breaking of Barriers in American Music*. Philadelphia: Temple University Press, 2014.

Cloud, Suzanne, and David Dzubinski, ed. *Philadelphia Real Book*. Philadelphia: Temple University Press, 2022.

Gillespie, Dizzy, and Al Fraser. *To Be, or Not...to Bop*. New York: Doubleday, 1979.

Golson, Benny, and Jim Merod. *Whisper Not: The Autobiography of Benny Golson*. Philadelphia: Temple University Press, 2016.

Heath, Jimmy, and Joseph McLaren. *I Walked with Giants: The Autobiography of Jimmy Heath*. Philadelphia: Temple University Press, 2010.

Porter, Lewis. *John Coltrane: His Life and Music*. Ann Arbor: University of Michigan Press, 1998.

Szwed, John F. *Space is the Place: The Lives and Times of Sun Ra*. New York: Pantheon Books, 1997.

Turner, Diane D. *Feeding the Soul: Black Music, Black Thought*. Chicago: Third World Press, 2011.

www.ingramcontent.com/pod-product-compliance
Lightning Source LLC
LaVergne TN
LVHW071932040926
847296LV00039B/480
* 9 7 8 1 4 6 7 1 0 7 8 4 6 *